8 Ways to Say "I Love My Life!"

8 Ways to Say *"I Love My Life!"*

AUTHORS:
Nancy De Los Santos Reza
Josefina López
Margo De León
Laura De Anda
Susan Orosco
Bel Hernandez Castillo
Joanna Ilizaliturri Díaz
Rita Mosqueda Marmolejo

FOREWORD BY Vikki Carr
EDITED BY Sylvia Mendoza

"Powerful stories of eight remarkable Latinas"
— from the foreword by Vikki Carr

Arte Público Press
Houston, Texas

8 Ways to Say "I Love My Life!" is funded in part by a grant from the City of Houston through the Houston Arts Alliance.

Recovering the past, creating the future

Arte Público Press
University of Houston
4902 Gulf Fwy, Bldg 19, Rm 100
Houston, Texas 77204-2004

Cover design by Mora Des!gn
Cover photo by Angela María Ortíz S.

Mendoza, Sylvia, ed.
  8 Ways to Say "I Love My Life!" / edited by Sylvia Mendoza
     p. cm.
  ISBN 978-1-55885-754-4 (alk. paper)
    1. Women—Psychology. 2. Women in the professions—Biography. 3. Self-realization in women—Case studies. 4. Hispanic American women in mass media. I. Mendoza, Sylvia. II. Title: Eight ways to say "I love my life!".
HQ1206.A14 2012
155.3'33—dc23

                                             2012026152
                                                   CIP

∞ The paper used in this publication meets the requirements of the American National Standard for Information Sciences—Permanence of Paper for Printed Library Materials, ANSI Z39.48-1984.

©2012 by 8 Ways Life Group
Imprinted in the United States of America

12 13 14 15 16 17 18   10 9 8 7 6 5 4 3 2 1

Table of Contents

FOREWORD | Vikki Carr   vii

PREFACE | Susan Orosco   xi

ONE   1
Loving My Life
Nancy De Los Santos Reza

TWO   33
The Unlovable
Josefina López

THREE   61
The Pillar that Would Not Crumble
Margo De León

FOUR   87
My Father's Daughter
Laura De Anda

FIVE   111
The Clearing
Susan Orosco

SIX   143
The Power to Say I Belong
Bel Hernandez Castillo

SEVEN   167
¿Qué te dice tu corazón?
Joanna Ilizaliturri Díaz

EIGHT   195
Running in Place
Rita Mosqueda Marmolejo

Foreword

I AM HONORED TO WRITE THE FOREWORD FOR THIS life-changing, inspirational book, *8 Ways to Say "I Love My Life!"*

The powerful stories of eight remarkable Latinas tell how they overcame challenging odds to beat their personal demons. Their renewed spirit led them to a place where each could honestly say, "I love my life."

Every one of the eight stories deeply moved me. These tales filled with hope are not just for Latinas, but for all women (and men) who want their voices to go from weak to strong, and for the quality of their lives to move from a static state to full blossom. These stories can guide a reader's self-love to emerge from beneath insecurities and dark places. This emotional process struck a very familiar chord in me.

Being Vikki Carr is not for the weak or faint of heart. For many years, the time I spent on stage, singing to the loving spirit of my loyal fans was all I had that was truly mine and mine alone. Everything else in my young life was orchestrated by others whose mission was to groom me into an international performer and entertainer, a bright shining star. I was raised to tackle the task at hand, follow directions and not ask questions.

My father was the strong head of our household. Mother always knew and accepted her subservient place at his side. As the eldest of seven children, I was expected to shoulder the responsibility of helping with the cooking, cleaning and caring for my younger siblings. I was my mother's helping hand. I was brought up to respect and listen to my elders and never question them. As I grew older and went on the road with my music, I knew no other way. At home this was my safety net; away from home, it proved to be my vulnerability.

My journey, like each of these women's journeys, had its share of painful moments. There were times when life disappointed me, when people and events let me down. I began to doubt myself. One day, I took a good look at my life and realized I was stronger than what I gave myself credit for. Like the women in this book, I learned to fight for what I wanted and needed.

As I read their eloquently written words, I came to the realization that I am not alone, that none of us really are. Strength rose up inside of me as I continued to read their stories. Suddenly, the journeys and adventures I thought were so unique to my life experiences were not. What a blow to my ego! But what an amazing realization: We are all sisters, *hermanas*, wanting to have a life filled with love. I was moved by the many messages this book conveys so beautifully, yet reinforces how I do not accept excuses and strongly believe we need to take responsibility for our own lives. We can make our own dreams come true.

"My Father's Daughter," written by Laura De Anda, touched me deeply. It deals with guilt mixed with family and fear, especially fear of her father's illness. Like the author, I've learned that guilt is something we must let go of in order to succeed. Your life is about you, the things you feel and what you know is right for you—but sometimes we just need to let go.

The strength of each of these women shines through in their stories. Josefina López learns that her life and her love can be on her own terms. Nancy De Los Santos Reza finds power in accepting responsibility for her life, then chooses what she feels is best for her. Bel Hernandez Castillo finds her voice through the strength in her identity as Chicana: her Mexican and American roots. Margo De León realizes that forgiveness is the key to inner peace and a life filled with love and joy. Susan Orosco changes the course of her life from a self-destructive path to seeking the meaning of her life and how God fits in. Rita Mosqueda Marmolejo finds recovery from a legacy of addiction and mental illness. And, Joanna Díaz emulates the strong women in her life to find her place in this world. In each of these examples, a loving source from within pulled them up.

We all have our challenges in life; mine is to see my self-worth. It took me a long time to acknowledge it. In one night I could easily go from singing to the Queen of England or the President of the United States to slipping into a period of self-doubt as I fell asleep. Like many others before me, I went in search of answers from God or "The Universe" to my most perplexing questions. Whatever you call Him, He hears all prayer. It took me a while to learn that. Being Catholic, I have found the place where I truly belong.

If I could help someone heal their life through sharing my life lessons, the greatest lesson would be that you never lose God. Not once did God forsake me, nor take His love and support from me. As I learned to value myself, I realized that God's gifts are bountiful. In my heart I know He created me and gave me a very special gift that I share with the world. He gave all of us "free will" along with many other blessings. Some of us do not listen to our inner voice at times and we continue to make the same mistakes over and over again. It is only when we finally say, "¡Basta! ¡Ya!" that we finally choose Him over everything else. That's precisely the moment when we let go. For me that moment came when I took a deep breath and said, "I'm all yours God. Let's go."

Often, the big question begs to be asked about all our lives: Would I change anything? My answer is, probably not. These were the life lessons I had to learn over and over again, until I finally "got" them. I did that by having faith, being still and letting my inner voice guide me. And this is what each of the *8 Ways to Say "I Love My Life!"* women have learned. Listen to your own voice.

You will find that the beautiful narratives in this wonderful book say all of this and more. Eight marvelous Latinas overcame the boundaries and limits imposed upon them, fought being wrongly stereotyped and were not afraid to ask for what they wanted in life and fight for it. Each of them listened to her inner voice, which had been there all along, waiting for the chance to shout, "Hey, world! Look at me! I love my life!" And I join them!

Besos y abrazos,
Vikki Carr

Preface

8 WAYS TO SAY "I LOVE MY LIFE!" WAS BORN IN MY BACKYARD. On a beautiful summer evening, my husband and I sat by the pool drinking Santa Margherita's Pinot Grigio. We were celebrating the new greenhouse he had built for me to house my tropical plants. It was a marvelous addition to our already beautiful backyard. When I finished the last drop of wine from my goblet, he asked if I wanted more. I nodded contentedly. Then my husband stood up from the patio table, held up his arms, looked up to the sky and declared, "I love my life!"

When he walked inside the house, I sat there, contemplating what had just happened. I felt excitement, surprise but most of all, jealousy. I wanted what he had. I wanted to be able to stand up and declare to the heavens that they had done a good job with my life. I wanted to shout to the world, I love my life! Most of all I wanted to mean it, and say it with conviction. I wanted to love my life not in spite of what I had been through but because of it.

So every morning before lunch and in the evening I began to affirm, "I love my life." At first, it felt odd especially when I held my arms in the air, but it felt magnificent. I didn't believe my life was perfect; therefore it was hard to love it at first. But I continued to affirm it. After each session, I noticed I felt more energized and excited about life. After a week, I noticed I was remembering good things that had happened to me.

I realized that loving my life was like loving a spouse. It needed attention, recognition and appreciation. My life and I were having a love affair that required respect, communication and acceptance. After the second week, I noticed everything that had ever happened to me in my life started to make sense.

I told my friend Margo De León about my experience. I wanted her to begin the journey of loving her life so she too could reap the benefits. I also told her I wanted to write a book called "How to Say "I Love my Life"... and Mean It!" I asked if she wanted to write it with me. She agreed.

Margo improved upon my idea. She told me she always wanted to write a book with other Latinas. I thought that was a great idea. I had thought about writing the book with other women but I had not thought to make it a Latina project.

We decided to invite five additional authors: Laura De Anda, Nancy De Los Santos Reza, Bel Hernandez Castillo, Joanna Ilizaliturri Díaz and Rita Mosqueda Marmolejo. They were chosen for their ability to write, speak publicly and to pursue an authentic life. Through our selection process, we ended up losing one author and gaining two more because Nancy invited the eighth author, Josefina López.

At first, Margo and I agonized about what to do with eight stories when our plans were to have only seven. Laura suggested we keep all eight for several reasons. The number eight symbolizes power, abundance and luck. Also not only does the symbol 8 represent eternity; it even looks like the shape of a woman. We smiled and agreed.

We held one of our first meetings at Josefina's theater, Casa 0101, in Boyle Heights. I remember when I approached the theater, seeing the sign on the door informing us the meeting place had been moved down the street. It read "8 Ways to Say I Love My Life meeting will be held at . . . " and she gave the address. Later, when I mentioned to her the correct title ("How to Say 'I Love my Life'... and Mean It!") she said she didn't know how she had made that mistake. It turned out we all really liked the new title and so it stayed. I envisioned the tagline: "8 Women. 8 Stories. 8 Miracles."

After the meeting, Josefina suggested we take excerpts from the chapters that we were still working on and create monologues to be presented at her theater for "Women's He*r*story Month." It was a challenging idea since March was just a few months away, but we agreed. It was exciting to see how we all came together to produce the monologues. Josefina held a monologue writing class and, with her husband Emmanuel Deleage's help, our autobiographical stories were ready to be presented onstage. Emmanuel would direct six of the monologues and Hector Rodriguez directed the other two. Auditions were held and seven actresses were hired to perform one monologue each while Rita chose to perform her own.

Our first meeting to hear the actresses read was one of the most amazing experiences I had ever had. It was spellbinding to hear the words we had written come alive with the depth of an actor's soul as each portrayed our lives. I made note of the reactions of each author and could tell from the look of astonishment on their faces that I was not the only one who knew something magical was happening.

The monologues drew packed houses for a two-week run. A couple of months later, after popular demand, we produced the monologues again at the Los Angeles Theater Center with Diane Rodriguez as director. Again we had a packed house plus a favorable review in the *Los Angeles Times*.

Soon after that, we were nominated for the Imagen Award, which is a competitive award from the Imagen Award Foundation. Also known as the Latino Golden Globes, the Imagen Awards gala is held in Beverly Hills and honors the best and most positive portrayals of Latinos in entertainment.

To be honest, being nominated with other stage productions that were heavy hitters with larger budgets was enough of an honor for me, but not for the monologues. No, as I said before, the monologues had developed a life of their own, and emerged as winners.

On August 2009 we won the Imagen Award for Best Live Theatrical Production. Our beautiful trophy sits at Josefina's theater in Boyle Heights.

After all this delicious commotion the time came for us to buckle down and finish our chapters. We needed to complete the manuscript so we could submit it and find a literary agent.

As we each wrote our chapters, we began to feel like cracked eggs. We felt broken, revealing to each other our innermost demons, pains and strengths. We were talking and writing about love, family and our personal lives. And for some of us that was a touchy subject. At times, our meetings started to become strained. I think most of us were not used to being so vulnerable.

On several occasions, we simply needed time out. But we kept going. I think what inspired us was the success of the monologues, with their critical acclaim and the incredible audience reception. Our stories were helping people; they were healing. Most especially, we were healing.

Just when we thought our chapters couldn't get any better, Laura suggested we hire an editor. She found Sylvia Mendoza. Handing over our 'babies' to her was not easy for us, but we trusted her.

Sylvia took our tear-stained manuscript and dug even deeper. I soon realized she was one of those writers who believed a good manuscript had to have more than tears; it needed blood, too. So be it. She took a red pen and, wow, did we bleed. But the chapters were sharper, clearer and the message was driven home. Sylvia understood what we were trying to say because she was of like mind.

Everything that was happening, the monologues, Sylvia, the chapters were doing a number on the eight of us. We were growing, learning and healing. It was painful and exhilarating at the same time. It was lot like giving birth.

I used to believe that the power of intention was the strongest spiritual tool. But during this process I learned that the power of decision was even stronger. My understanding of the word intention is wanting something to happen. But to decide was to put it in motion. If we did not love our lives before this project; we certainly would afterward because we decided we would. The writing of our stories led us onto that path.

I wrote the proposal for the manuscript and began the tedious process of submitting it to a list of agents that specialized in the genre of our collected essays. My intention was to submit exclusively to each agent, so that meant waiting for a rejection or a reasonable amount of time with no response, before submitting to the next name on the list. The first agent I submitted to, responded within a week. She passed on the project but she liked the idea and wished us the best of luck. I went on to the second on the list and this time, she asked for the manuscript. Leticia Gomez became our agent.

Margo and I had a pow-wow about our book nearly every day. I kept saying we needed another Latina to write a foreword to the book. I wanted a big name. Not so big that her contract wouldn't allow it (which was the case with Eva Longoria), yet big enough to be known nationwide. I thought of Vikki Carr, La Bikki.

Margo assured me it wouldn't hurt to ask. The worst that could happen is she could say no. Two days later, Vikki responded to my email. She wanted to see the manuscript. Margo and I jumped for joy because we knew once she saw the manuscript; she would love it. Margo and I gave thanks to the heavens for yet another miracle.

Several months later, Leticia found our publisher Arte Público Press, and the rest of the story is found in the book you hold in your hands. This book is a dream come true, and a blessing. It is a gift from eight women who have shared their life lessons, their tears and joys, so you may fully enjoy your own journey.

We believe that loving your life is not about waiting until your life gets better before you can love it. When you learn to love your life, you learn to love yourself and to love others. For example, my husband and I will celebrate ten years of marriage. What is amazing is that the more I love my life; my love for him grows stronger. Any flaws seem insignificant in comparison to the love I hold in my heart.

Loving your life is about reclaiming *you*, the authentic you. Choosing to love your life does not mean there is no room for improvement in your life, it just means you are willing to begin the love affair and are willing to notice and enjoy what is right with your life and, most importantly, what is right with you. This is your miracle waiting to happen.

Susan Orosco
www.8waystosay.com

> **NANCY DE LOS SANTOS REZA** is a writer, playwright, documentary filmmaker and producer. She is the associate producer of the films *Selena* and *My Family, Mi Familia*. She has written for The Disney Channel, Showtime, PBS and Lifetime. She is co-writer and co-producer of the HBO documentary *The Bronze Screen: 100 Years of the Latino Image in Hollywood Cinema*. Born and raised in Chicago, Nancy began her career as producer for Roger Ebert and Gene Siskel's film review program *At the Movies*. She is a member of the Writers Guild of America and co-founded The Wise Latina Society. Nancy is thankful for a great life and grateful for her terrific *esposo*, Daniel Reza.
> www.NancyDeLosSantos.com
> www.TheWiseLatinaSociety.com

Loving My Life

I'VE LOVED MY LIFE EVER SINCE I COULD REMEMBER even thinking about loving my life, but that's not saying my life has been a big bowl of *pozole* (a traditional Mexican corn stew). I've been through the 'What-the-heck-was-I-thinking? stage' after life-changing decisions threw me off course more than a few times. I've experienced the depression of young heartbreak and the agony of adult heartache and can tell you this: a broken heart is a heart broken in a thousand pieces at any age. I've been shaken by the realization that if I was going do anything of note in my life, I would most likely have to leave my family and hometown and do it on my own.

Through it all, I've loved my life because I have lived my life as I have chosen. I've learned that only I am responsible for my life: the good, the bad, the positive, the negative, successes and failures. They all belong to me. They are the result of my decisions, my choices. Once I realized that my life truly meant *my* life, I could say "I love my life" and mean it.

No one who knew me growing up on Chicago's South Side in a Mexican-American working-class family—one of six children and a member of a Latina girl gang—would ever have imagined that I would graduate from two respected universities, have a successful career in television, work on major Hollywood film productions and travel internationally for work and pleasure.

In fact, those who knew me told me quite differently. The principal of my elementary school—a very scary nun—warned my parents, "She's going to be pregnant before she's sixteen and drop out of school!" Instead, I graduated first in my class and was awarded a scholarship. A colleague at my high school part-time job in a department store said there was no need to train me; I would eventually quit to have a "boatload of kids, like all the other Mexican girls." Instead, I learned about birth control, rose to supervisor and became a respected member of the staff. A college counselor told me that at twenty-four I was, "Too old to begin college." Instead, I enrolled and earned a Bachelor of Science degree in Radio, Television and Film, and a Master's degree in Communications.

Add to that my embracing of New Thought spirituality and finding true love on the internet, and the result is one very surprising life that I can truly say I love.

Sometimes it's not what you do that makes your life lovable, but what you *didn't* do. I didn't drop out of school and get pregnant, as so many expected. I didn't marry when I was a teen, as I had planned to do. I didn't stay in the girl gang, as many of my friends did. And, I didn't stay in my hometown, as almost everyone I grew up with did.

I broke tradition and kept the pieces that fit me. I took chances and marveled that I survived. I sacrificed security for adventure. The result is a life that was different from any I had seen as a young girl.

All this began as a wish of a twelve-year-old girl. It was my birthday. I remember looking around my neighborhood and my family, and seeing women who didn't seem very happy with their lives: mothers raising too many children, often alone, young women with so much potential, but still working in menial jobs. The only women of any stature in my community were the Catholic school nuns.

Don't get me wrong. Many of the women I knew were brave, tenacious, and had gumption. I saw flashes of their creativity, their quest for knowledge and meaningful lives while they raised children, kept a household, held down an outside job and were supportive wives. I wanted to emulate their positive traits and leave behind what didn't work for me.

I knew I didn't want to be controlled or stifled or limited by tradition, society, husbands or boyfriends. And I didn't hear angels sing when I thought of being a nun. So, on May 10 of my twelfth year on the planet, I stood as still as a statue and wished for a life that would be different. I didn't have the foggiest idea of what "different" meant, but I knew that's what I wanted. What I've learned is that sometimes the rewards of being different are great and sometimes the price is loneliness and self doubt. I discovered what is best for me by seeking information and making my own choices. Perhaps my lessons learned will aid you in understanding how to love your own life and embrace it.

Know Your Roots

Who are your parents? First generation immigrants? Fifth generation, native born? If they left their homeland, what were their reasons? What were their experiences as youngsters, teenagers, adults? How were they treated by their own parents? By society? Were they raised in an inclusive community or were they excluded? How did they respond to their environment? Take the time to discover the what, why and how of your parents' lives and their parents' lives. You'll find yourself in the answers.

The decisions our families made come full circle in our lives and bring us to this point in the universe where we now stand. Knowing your familial roots and your ancestors' decisions can offer great insight into who you are today.

My maternal grandmother, Soledad Gallegos, was a beautiful and brave woman. Born in Zacatecas, Mexico, barely 15 years old when the economic toll of the Mexican Revolution forced her mother, Dominga, to gather her four daughters and travel to the United States. I can imagine these two women with their young charges traveling during this tumultuous time across one country to another, sometimes on horseback or mule, maybe on a train, and most likely, walking. Somehow my great-grandmother Dominga and my grandmother Soledad arrived with their family in Eastland, Texas, about 100 miles outside of Dallas. What I know for sure is that whatever chances I have taken in my life pale in comparison to these two women traveling with young children from a country ravaged by war to a country foreign in every way. I believe the seeds of my adventure-loving soul surely were sowed by my brave *abuelita*.

Soledad met her first husband in Texas and had two children with him. He worked for the railroad, but was fired after being accused of stealing. He left town, promising to return when things cooled down. Months turned into years. Soledad placed personal ads in the Spanish-language newspaper, hoping for a response from her husband, but she never heard from him again. A few years later, a young, strong, Polish man working as a mason, arrived in town. Felix Arkiemenski had traveled from Nova Scotia, Canada, to Texas to work on the construction of a local dam. There, Felix shortened his name to Arkie and found Soledad, ten years his junior. Although she didn't speak Polish and he didn't speak much Spanish, they married and brought five children into this world.

In Eastland, Soledad's Polish-Mexican children were labeled "half-breeds" and were shunned by both the Mexicans *and* the Anglos. Micaela, my mother, was, and still is, quite a beauty—with flashing green eyes that can console you one minute and in the next send a shiver of fear up your spine. She and her siblings were raised in a small home built by their father on the outskirts of town. As a young girl, she picked cotton with her family and happily tended to the family's cows and goats. Her eyes welled up whenever she told the sad story of one of her pets, a goat she loved. When the family needed it, the pet became their dinner. I inherited her love for animals and have always had a dog in my home.

I'm told Grandfather Felix was a master masonry worker and a world-class drinker. By the time he was in his early forties, he developed cirrhosis of the liver. This was right after World War II. Soledad's oldest daughter, Luz, had moved to Chicago, in search of work in the city's factories. Her two sons had also moved to the city of big shoulders. Felix died, Soledad took her three youngest daughters to join her older children. Soledad, like her mother before her, traveled to a new land to find work and create a new home for her family.

This time it would be the Windy City.

My grandmother's brave decision to move more than a thousand miles from a town of hundreds to a city of hundreds of thousands gave me and all her grandchildren an opportunity to create lives filled with possibilities.

My father, Nicolás De Los Santos, one of sixteen children, was also born and raised in Eastland. At seventeen, he joined the Navy during World War II, following the path of seven of his brothers who served in every branch of the service. One brother was killed in Normandy; another was a prisoner of war in Nazi Germany. Eight De Los Santos brothers in the military during this war garnered his mother, Angelita De Los Santos, the honor of being named "Texas Mother of the Year."

A handsome man with a dazzling smile, he was always ready with a joke and an offer of a beer. My dad was a genius car and truck mechanic. He was sought out at his job by the truck drivers who wanted the best. He was of that first generation of Mexican-American men who worked outside of their Latino community; I believe that affected his life. The company offered him a promotion to daytime supervisor, but Daddy chose to stay on the graveyard shift as a mechanic. I didn't understand his choice not to accept the promotion, but I've learned to understand his choices. I've experienced doubts about my own abilities, fear has sometimes held me back, but knowing that my parents sacrificed much in order for me to have the chance to succeed, I choose to quiet those doubts with action.

My father's work ethic was as strong as the city we call home. I can't remember one evening when he didn't go to work—no matter rain, sleet or snow. One winter, Chicago experienced a dreadful snowstorm. Over three feet of the white stuff covered the city, shutting down schools, businesses and city services. There was so much snow that my brothers were jumping off the second story porch into immense snow drifts that almost reached the porch. The streets and highways were closed, but that didn't matter to my father. He walked the five miles to work, saying, "Got to get the trucks ready to roll tomorrow." My work ethic is reflected in his words.

My father working on the night shift left most of the parenting to my mother; a big job for any one person. When I close my eyes and think back to my childhood, I see my mother surrounded by her six children, all of them crying and fighting, vying for her attention. She gave each of us the time needed to make us feel special. My special times with her were spent taking in a rare matinee. To this day, I consider a matinee to be a particularly sweet treat. My mother didn't work outside our home until my youngest brother was in high school. When we returned from school, she was always home with a snack and a question,

"What did you learn today?" This one question kept me alert throughout the day, knowing that I had better pay attention in school and have something to report!

I also grew up with two grandmothers in my life, *dos abuelitas*, both of whom were strong life forces.

Soledad Gallegos Arkie was a great woman with a name that reflected a new American generation of mixed cultures. "Soledad" translates to "solitude," but she was the center of our family; a short tower of strength, tenacity and love. She lived with my family, sleeping on a twin bed in what would have been a dining room in our third-floor walk-up apartment. My sleepy eyes watched her wake up at three a.m. to take a city bus to her commercial bakery job, returning in the early afternoon with a few of the factory's fried fruit pies. Somewhere in her busy schedule, Grandma Soledad found time to make tall stacks of tortillas. Nothing has ever tasted as good as one of her hot-off-the-*comal* flour tortillas with a dab of butter.

She worked her factory job for twenty-five years and every payday, Abuelita paid her *biles*—her share of the rent, the light bill, the gas bill. With any money left, she bought necessities for her grandchildren. Every winter coat I ever had was bought by Grandma. She possessed a great faith in the Catholic Church, the Virgen de Guadalupe and Jesucristo. An altar with her *santos* and photos of family adorned an ancient pedal sewing machine next to her bed. She prayed the rosary every evening, but still visited with the local *curandero* when she needed direct action. Her spiritual faith paved the road of my spiritual life. From my grandmother, I've learn to respect the Catholic Church and to find my own faith. And I've visited a *curandero* or two. Grandma taught me that faith in whatever we chose to believe is one of our strongest allies.

I love the translation of my paternal grandmother's name, Angelita De Los Santos: Little Angel of the Saints. But she was no delicate angel, she had the strength of an archangel. In 1939, Angelita's beloved husband, Ernesto, died from a massive heart attack. Angelita knew she had to figure out a way for her family to survive. With ten of her sixteen children still at home, the family went on the migrant trail to the Midwest. this seasonal work took many Mexican-American families from Texas to the farms in Michigan, Illinois and Indiana to pick cherries, cucumbers and lettuce. During this time, World War II broke out, and eight of the De Los Santos brothers, including my dad, joined the war effort. The family returned Eastland at the end of the war to welcome home their sons and brothers who had served in the military. Realizing there was very little work available in Texas, Angelita made the decision to move her family to Chicago.

Abuelita Angelita was an entrepreneur at heart. She knew that where there were workers, there would be paychecks—and the need to spend those checks for a little fun on a Friday night. In the early 1950s, she opened a bar and restaurant in Chicago that catered to Mexicans and Mexican Americans. The business establishments were rowdy, loud and fun. So much fun, that my father often "forgot" to return home from a visit. My mother never learned to drive and, saddled with six children, had little choice but to wait for him to return in his own time.

The lesson from that observation was not to allow anyone to have control over my life—or my transportation. I learned to drive as soon as I turned fifteen.

While my parents did argue, I never saw my father strike my mother. Their arguments were just that: verbal matches filled with threats, sometimes accompanied by flying objects—shoes, pots and pans. All my siblings swear to witnessing my mother, on one particular Christmas Eve, hoisting the decorated tree acrosss the living room onto my father's head. No matter how much he yelled, my mother always yelled back. My mother's strength as a woman has given me strength. "Meek" is not a word ever used to describe my mother or me, or my sisters Gloria and Rose. Like my mother, my two sisters will do whatever is necessary to protect their children and themselves. None of us will back down from an argument, which is both a blessing and a curse, take the case of the pan of hot frying shrimp. A college boyfriend continued to argue with me while I was cooking. Maybe he was right. We went back and forth, until the line was crossed. I picked up the pan of sizzling shrimp and threw it at him. Thankfully, I missed. But you get the picture. I don't condone my actions. I'm just saying, we learn from our mothers. A lot.

No matter how many arguments, my parents stayed together until my father's death, through almost forty years of marriage. Some of those years were marred with accusations of my father's infidelity. My mother may have had proof of his indiscretions, but somehow their love for each other and for their children always mattered more in the end. "Divorce" was a word thrown about many times, but never realized. It took some time and some professional counseling for me to understand my parents' relationship. Their love for each other and their children was their life anchor.

My parents' commitment to their marriage gave me both the belief that marriage is a lifetime commitment *and* the desire to find the absolute right person to make that commitment. The lesson was to do whatever I could to be sure to marry the right man, the man who could stand next to me and say, "Let's do this. Together." Finding him took some work. Keeping him and the marriage takes some more work, but it's worth it.

Being born into this working-class Mexican-American family was a rewarding experience. We ate spaghetti and meatballs on Sundays and made tamales on Christmas. We had peanut butter sandwiches for lunch, but there were always tortillas *de harina hechas a mano* in the kitchen. We spoke English at home as a direct result of my parents' mistreatment as children speaking Spanish at their Texas schools. We spoke broken Spanish to our *abuelitas*. While there was food on the table and a roof over our heads, we definitely lived paycheck to paycheck. I'm grateful for a mother who expected each of us to do well in school and a father with a strong work ethic. I'm fortunate to have had a childhood where those basics were supplied, along with many life lessons on love and commitment.

Don't Let Your History Hold You Back

Know your family's history, then using that wonderful gift of free will decide what you'd like to take with you as you grow into your own life. Too often I've thought that I could not do something or be something because of who I am. Mexican. Mexican American. It hurts me to say, but it's true. My unexamined interpretation of my history supplied what I now see as excuses for not moving forward. "I can't write. No one in my family writes. I don't know any Mexicans who write." "I can't go to college. No one I know goes to college. No one in my family graduated high school. I don't know any Mexican Americans who have gone to college."

All that, it turns out, is complete and utter nonsense. Baseless excuses. As a matter of fact, one of my aunts, Lita De Los Santos, is a writer, having in her late 70s, published two family memoirs, with another in the works.

I might not have known any Mexicans who wrote or went to college, but I do know Mexicans who bravely risked their lives to travel thousands of miles in order to provide a better life for their families. I know Mexican-American women who unselfishly worked from sunrise to sunset at factory jobs or at their own corner tavern or neighborhood restaurant. I might not have known any Mexicans who were writers, but my *tíos* could sing hundreds of songs by memory and create new ones on a whim. I knew *tías* who could weave stories that would mesmerize a roomful of unruly children. I did know Mexican-American families who creatively fed huge families on very small paychecks and still had something left over for a Sunday treat. That takes talent.

Latinos have a rich history. While Europeans were living in huts, our ancestors in this hemisphere had sophisticated cultures, built magnificent cities, created incredible art and developed intricate languages and mathematical concepts. The cities of Aztecs, Mayans and Incas still stand as a confirmation to their ingenuity, intelligence and natural curiosity.

Growing up Mexican American in Chicago during my time—and probably for a long time after that—meant not knowing one single thing about this history. In fact, this great history was hidden, trashed and maligned into some kind of mishmash of stereotypes that included the *bandido*, the sexy *señorita*, the wild *indio*. As a group, we were considered "less than." There were no expectations to achieve. There were no invitations to success. Our history was not taught and definitely not honored. As a young girl I asked my mother, "What are we?" Her answer: "Spanish." It was not until I was in college that I realized I was not Spanish. I was Mexican, Mexican American, and as I learned about our history and became politically aware, I decided on my self-label, Chicana.

In high school I joined a storefront neighborhood community group, Mujeres Latinas en Acción, and learned that we—all Latinos—were so much more than what I knew. This incredible group of female leaders, some gifted with education, others only steeped in the ways of the street, encouraged me and other young women in our neighborhood to learn about our history. My first trip out of the country was with Mujeres Latinas to Mexico City, Distrito Federal, México, for The International Women's Day Conference. Once I stepped onto the "Pyramid of the Sun" in Teotihuacán and looked out on the magnificent horizon, I knew I was special. I knew I had a legacy of many generations of scholars, teachers and artists. As I learned about our wonderful history, I held it tight, like a shield of honor.

Know your history and choose from the glorious past what you want to take with you on your own road. The Aztecs of Mexico. The Taínos of Puerto Rico. The Mayas of Central America. The Incas of South America. Realize that each Latino family has something special that has been handed down. Know it and embrace it.

The support of a good group of people is like a free gift. Join like-minded people in their quest for change and knowledge and growth. There's power in a group of people with the same goal.

Find Your Spiritual Center and Live It

My mother was raised Catholic and raised her children Catholic. The benefit of that decision is that my siblings and I received a great education in Catholic elementary school. My father was raised a Baptist. His father, it's told, sometimes taught the word of the Bible. I never saw my father attend a church service, Baptist or Catholic. His religion was fishing, baseball, football and family. I completely understand his seeing God on a still lake at sunrise, waiting for the fish to bite. My mom would take us to church while Dad made Sunday *caldo de res*. It worked for them.

For my brothers and sisters, my parents agreed: Catholic school was a must. They scrimped and sacrificed to send us there. We moved into an Italian American neighborhood, on the same street where one of my mother's sisters lived with her German American husband. Chicago was a segregated city during this time, and there were only a few Mexican families living in this community. My German Mexican cousins were light-skinned and blue-eyed, and they easily fit into the neighborhood. Even my older brother did well; he had inherited my maternal grandfather's blue eyes. But me . . . I took after my father: dark skin, dark eyes, definitely Mexican, and didn't quite fit in. The landlord rented the apartment to us because he knew my aunt and uncle.

I will always be grateful to my parents for their sacrifice and the solid educational foundation received at the hands (and wooden rulers) of the Franciscan nuns. But, there were only three Mexican-American families in the parish, which accounted for about fifteen students, including me and my siblings. In this environment, I received an unexpected education in the ways of the world and institutional racism.

In seventh grade, at the age of fourteen, I had a crush on a boy who was older than me by three years. He was a junior in high school and drove his own car. I can't blame the nuns for having a fit when he rolled up in his yellow Chevy and parked in front of the elementary school every day at three o'clock. Young and foolish, we were actually making plans to get married as soon as he graduated from high school! I can't blame the nuns for insisting to my mother that I take the part-time job they offered, which placed me in the parish rectory from school's dismissal at 3:15 to 8:00 in the evening every day.

I am, in fact, grateful they insisted I work at this after-school job. Looking back, I can see the benefits and the drawbacks of this arrangement. I worked in the rectory kitchen with the Italian cook and learned at her ample side how to make the perfect red sauce. At six o'clock sharp, the pastor with his two assistant priests sat at the formal dining room table and rang a bell, the signal for me to serve dinner, pour beverages, then wait in the kitchen until the bell was rung again to remove their plates, serve coffee and, usually, a dessert of Italian cannoli.

During this time, I was experimenting with black eyeliner and pink lipstick, wore a plaid parochial school uniform skirt rolled up into a mini, a white pressed blouse and knee socks. I never suspected I was having any effect on anyone's thoughts, but I was.

After dinner, the cook went home, and I was left to wash the dishes and mop the kitchen floor. Then I sat in the church office to complete my homework while answering the rectory's phone and greeting parishioners who needed copies of birth, death or marriage certificates. I was very proud of my job and pleased with the twenty dollars a week I was paid for the twenty-five hours of work.

It took many years before I could smell cigar smoke and not think of "Father S." He was young compared to our pastor, an elderly gentleman who promptly went to sleep after dinner. Father S. was in his early thirties and was probably troubled. I would smell the smoke from his evening cigar before I'd hear the stairs creak as he left his quarters on the third floor and walked into the rectory office, where I sat at a small wooden desk.

He'd approach me from behind, always quietly, always slowly, and place his hands on my shoulders, massaging them while uttering mindless small talk, "How are we doing tonight?"

I didn't have any idea what was on his mind. Although I did have that older boyfriend—that's what got me into the after-school rectory job to begin with—I was a good Catholic girl and had gone only as far as venial sin would allow.

"Have we had any phone calls?" he'd ask. I'd shrug, hard enough to get his hands off my shoulders. "Need any help with your homework?" I'd always answer "no" in a respectful tone. Nothing more than those pitiful moments marred my days at the rectory, and I can only thank whatever *santos* were protecting me. Later, I learned that Father S. had been transferred a number of times to other parishes and finally sent to a home for troubled priests.

That last year in elementary school should have been a great year for me. I had consistently been named to the honor roll, a feat not readily recognized by my father. Although, once, while fetching him from the corner tavern, I overheard him bragging to his friends of my scholastic feats. "My daughter's number one in the class! She's a really smart girl!" It was strange to hear his voice filled with pride. To this day, I can conjure up that feeling of joy I experienced hearing him speak with pride about me. Maybe that's why I was so angry when my scholastic accomplishments were not embraced by the school's administrators.

It was the school's tradition to award the title of "First Girl" and "First Boy" to the students who scored the highest on our final exams. The title came with a four-year scholarship to an area

Catholic high school. That year, I had garnered the highest test scores and was ready to be named First Girl. I expected that honor. The expense of parochial high school was beyond my parents' limited budget; this was the only way I could attend a Catholic high school. When it was announced that for the first time, the four-year scholarship would be *shared* by the first- and second-place girls, an Italian American girl and me, I felt cheated. Each of us received funds to cover two years' tuition.

My experience with Catholic elementary and high school had little effect on my decision not to continue in the Catholic religious tradition as an adult. All along I had questioned the teachings and beliefs. When I discovered how babies were made, I just couldn't wrap my ten-year-old head around the virgin birth. I asked the nuns questions, but could never get a straight answer. Traveling to Mexico with Mujeres Latinas en Acción as a teenager, I would not believe that a good, just God would harbor anger against women who used birth control. There were too many women living in poverty, burdened with more children than they could care for and feed. How could a loving God send them to eternal damnation for using a condom? Many people still believe in these tenets of the Church and I respect their beliefs. But I also believe it is senseless for us mere mortals to argue about whose man-made religion is right. God is God. Religion is a choice.

I still pray to a few saints. My Grandma Soledad's favorite *santo* was St. Jude, the patron saint of workers and "all things impossible." I like the idea that there's someone out there rooting for the impossible to be possible! I sometimes attend mass at a beautiful little church near my home, believing God is everywhere, and I applaud the good works the Catholic Church does worldwide.

However, I believe there is a power that is greater than all of us, a power that we are a part of and that is a part of us. I believe in the Universal force that we can tap into for our own good and the good of others. I began studying New Thought metaphysics with the Science of Mind spiritual organization founded by Ernest Holmes, and embraced this movement that believes all roads lead to God, Spirit, Universe. Spirituality is important in my life. Meditation, prayer, thanksgiving and reflection are all daily desires, if not actions.

Attending Sunday service gives me a few good words to live my week. Having our own spiritual center reminds us that we are all part of a much bigger picture. Find yours and embrace it.

Make Interesting Choices and Make Them Your Own

I attended the Catholic girls' high school for two years on that "First Girl" scholarship, making trouble all the way, quickly realizing I didn't want to be there. The mostly Irish and Italian student body certainly did not welcome me or the few black and Puerto Rican students I befriended. They didn't like us, and we didn't like them. The local boys, however, ignored the cultural divide, especially when it came to their raging hormones.

I learned to street fight because one Irish boy flirted with me and I flirted back. His Irish sweetheart called me out on it, and I had no choice but to meet her in the park on a cold autumn day and roll around on the fallen leaves, both of us kicking and scratching like mad women until a patrol car was sighted. I was recruited into our neighborhood's girl gang when more protection was deemed necessary.

The summer after graduation from elementary school was spent saying goodbye to that part of my life in many ways. The boyfriend I loved so much graduated from high school and returned to Mexico. Our plan was that he would come back to Chicago during the holidays, and we would get engaged for two years and then marry when I graduated.

Ah! Young love. My heartstrings tore soon after he left. I wanted to meet new people—and I discovered bad boys.

Bad boys are the bane of many women's lives. We just like them. No ifs, ands or buts about it. Most of us will have a bad boy or a few in our lives. Mine were members of the nearby neighborhood "club," the Spanish Chancellors. They were handsome. They had cars. They liked to dance. They were cool. My straitlaced Mexican boyfriend never had a chance.

How easily I went back and forth from parochial high school student to girl gang member. We were more of a club than a gang. The Spanish Chantels were the ladies auxiliary to the Spanish Chancellors. Basement parties, smoking cigarettes, heavy petting and lots of walking around the "hood" was about as dangerous as we got. The guys were a bit older than most of us, seventeen, maybe eighteen. They drank beer and shot pool in a rented storefront clubhouse that they paid for with part-time jobs. These were rather innocent times compared to anything that would happen in the future. Marijuana existed but was smoked only under heavy cover and considered too dangerous for girls. Instead, we drank sugar-sweet sloe gin with coke. What a sugar high! Fights between guys were fist to fist, and girl fights were hair pulling and blouse ripping extravaganzas. Slow dancing, making out and just hanging were how most of my gang-girl days were spent.

Teased hair, black eyeliner, white lipstick and that parochial school skirt rolled up at the waist created my "after-school uniform" that I wore with a club sweater. I suppose being in cold, windy Chicago made someone realize we needed sweaters. Every club had its own version of a club sweater. The Val Kyries, the Latin Queens and us, The Spanish Chantels, wore letterman-style sweaters—the type worn by Anglo male university students in old Mickey Rooney movies—black, hip-length, V-neck cardigans. Each club added a colored trim around the V, and on one side, an emblem with the club's name and symbol represented by—of all things—a coat of arms arbitrarily chosen from a book. On the other side, embroidered in big puffy letters was your nickname. The Spanish Chantels' color was a lively electric blue, and my puffy nickname stitched on the right side was "Smiles."

I paid for my club sweater with money I earned from babysitting jobs and hid that sweater from my mother under my mattress. To this day, I don't think she had any idea that I was leading a double life of Catholic School Girl and Girl Gang Member. That double life ended, rather abruptly, when I left Visitation Catholic Girls High School.

It was an interesting choice to join the girl gang, as was the choice to leave. While some might cringe at the thought, there were some great life lessons learned while a member of the Spanish Chantels. Loyalty, compassion and friendship are on top of the list. Days and evenings spent with other young teen girls, hearing their life stories, many who didn't have the two-parent foundation I did, let me know that I was blessed. I learned that even if a person makes a bad decision, she is entitled to a second chance—and can change her life if desire meets tenacity. I learned organizational skills as we planned basement birthday parties and military service going-away events. I experienced a camaraderie that only exists between people who feel they don't belong anywhere else but there.

I also had an inside view of life as a woman whose main man was in a gang, and I didn't like it. Many in this circle were pregnant by sixteen and dropped out of school to take care of their kids. They also worked outside the home, at whatever low-paying job they could get. Added to that, the guys were often thrown in jail for bad-boy actions of stealing cars, drinking in the street or fighting. While they were in "county"—the Cook County jail—their girls were expected to visit every Sunday. That meant dressing up in your best outfit, getting your child dressed up and taking the bus to 26th and California Avenue. They stood on the corner along with twenty or thirty other girls, shouting up to the windows of the jailhouse, while your man shouted back through the bars. The gang life had not reached the horrendous level of violence of recent times, but the life was not fun.

And I knew that life was not for me.

The two-year Catholic high school scholarship ended, and my parents had little choice but to send me to public high school. Most of the Latina and black teenage girls were funneled into one of the two local vocational public high schools. One taught cosmetology, the art of hair and make-up; the other was secretarial school offering classes in typing, office etiquette and grooming. There wasn't a single class on creative writing, music appreciation or Shakespearean literature between the two.

Most of my friends attended the hair and make-up school. I didn't have much interest in hairdos, but I wanted to be with my friends, and chose the cosmetology school. Then Abuelita Soledad had a talk with me. One day, while I waited for one of her tortillas *de harina* to be pulled off the hot *comal*, she said, "The secretaries at the factory always looked so nice in their office dresses—not sweaty and tired like me. I think you would be a very good secretary. You're smart. You can do that." As an enticement, she bought me a light blue manual typewriter with a matching carrying case. That was the clincher.

During this time, I also fell out of the Spanish Chantels. They considered me to be a square with a job. This was a definite fork in the road where I parted with most of my neighborhood girlfriends. It was difficult to leave the comfort of my neighborhood. I loved so much about it, and still do. But, that adventure-loving gene set in my soul by my grandmother said it was time to go and the excitement of something new out there on the horizon called to me.

I enrolled in the Jones Commercial High School near the downtown business center. The students rooted, not for a basketball or swim team, but for a typing team. The gym class consisted of learning to walk straight with a book balanced on your head. Typing and posture were stressed, not reading, not writing, not speaking. We were taught to take orders, not give them; to type proposals, not write them. I became a great secretary and a darn good typist.

The school was known for its dress code and "proper office wear" tradition. The few male students wore dress shirts and ties, along with dress shoes, pressed slacks and a suit jacket. Female students wore knee-length skirts or dresses. If your skirt length was questioned, you had to kneel on the floor. If the hem didn't touch the floor, you were sent home. Your hair could only reach your collar, but we were allowed to wear wigs if we wanted to keep our hair long. We were also required to wear—I'm afraid to say it, but it's true—hats and gloves to school. Hats and gloves and wigs! Oh my! Most girls put the hats and gloves on around the corner from the school, unrolled their mini skirts into longer versions, and strolled into the school, ready for class.

A saving grace of the school was the basic computer skills class offered. I was grateful for a class that challenged me. I became somewhat skilled at computer programming, and during my senior year, easily landed a part-time job at a small real estate firm.

Since the school accepted students from all over the city, I met many new nationalities, and my natural curiosity drew me into different circles. My new best friend was a tall, dishwater-blond Polish girl who grew up knowing only Polish people. We found the same things funny and enjoyed smoking cigarettes in the girls' lavatory.

At this point in my life, I knew, somewhere deep in my soul, that my birthday wish of long ago was coming true. My life would be different. And, I knew this would be because of the choices I would make. I would not be any of my girlfriends, who had all gotten pregnant and were left to care for their infants while their boyfriends continued to hang out, play pool and drink beer on the corner. I would not be any of the women in my neighborhood depending on a man to support them or a marriage that they felt was somehow the end-all.

I would not be any of the women I had seen in my life. Of course, I wanted to fall in love and get married. I had looked into the future and saw a life with a great husband and two or three lovely children. That perfect family didn't exist in my world. The young mothers I knew were mostly raising their children on their own. Food stamps and government assistance was their only support. If they *did* marry the baby's father, they struggled to make ends meet, juggling a part-time job and motherhood. Neither mother nor child was having a good life. I deduced that having children before you had a chance to get an education, experience life, find the right partner meant not living your life to its full potential. I wanted to make my life the best it could be.

As the oldest girl in my family, I had been a second mom to my younger siblings, learning early in life the responsibilities of motherhood. I watched my mom through four pregnancies and saw that becoming a mother took a lot of gumption, and being a mother demanded a boatload of work and sacrifice.

I didn't have the slightest idea of how I would find another life road, but I had a feeling that the choice of having or not having children would have a lot to do with it. I made a conscious decision not to become a single mother. I vowed not to have children until I was at least thirty and had been married to a wonderful man long enough to know he was going to stick around to be a good father. This meant taking care of myself, learning about birth control and using it.

But there was that one time, maybe two, perhaps more —parties, drinking, living in the moment, kisses that turned into passion—in which caution was thrown to the wind, that I managed to escape without becoming pregnant. I'm thinking prayer—a lot—helped. And there was that one time the birth control didn't work.

The copper coil was then a popular choice for birth control. Unfortunately, the coil inserted into me was defective. At nineteen, I became pregnant, but had no choice. The coil had to be removed, ending the pregnancy. That day remains a sad one in my life with many "what if's." But I do remember this. I took the bus to the after-hours medical clinic. The boyfriend picked me up after the procedure, on his motorcycle, and promptly dropped me off to make it to his nightly pool game at the corner tavern. I spent the evening alone and afraid. Soon after that, I made a decision to go to college and leave that boyfriend behind. And, I renewed my vow not to get pregnant until I was absolutely sure I was with the right guy.

The Mexican *dicho*, "Los hombres proponen, y Dios dispone" —People make plans, but God decides—says it all. I met that perfect guy almost twenty-five years later! He had raised his son, a terrific young man who had just graduated college, and felt it would be a challenge for him to start all over again with diapers and midnight feedings. But he offered to do it, if that's what I wanted.

Here it was. A major turning point in my life, a major decision. I thought about it. I prayed about it. I, we, decided, not to take the baby road. By this time in my life, I had realized there were many avenues to address any maternal need that I had. I'm a terrific and caring *tía*, and have been a committed Big Sister for a number of years. Working in my community, I offer young people whatever assistance and guidance I can whenever possible.

Having children must be a decision, not a lifestyle you fall into because that's what you think is expected of you, or because everyone is doing it.

Make bringing a life your life, a choice. Make being a mother a decision. And make this choice and this decision, yours.

Knock on Every Door

If you don't do anything, nothing will happen.

College was never a choice offered me, and I knew my family's financial support ended at my high school graduation. That was okay. Going to college was the furthest thing from my mind. I was a great typist (still am) and wanted a paycheck, not another report card. However, I didn't have *any* real knowledge about college. It was never discussed at secretarial school. I didn't know the difference between a BA, an MA or a PhD. It didn't matter. I wanted to work and make my own way in the world.

My first job was in the typing pool of a medical professional association. I was one of ten young women who spent the eight-hour day typing information onto forms. I loved it. A beautiful office on Chicago's famous Michigan Avenue. Lunch at the local deli with workmates. A Friday afternoon paycheck. I paid rent to my parents and spent the rest as I wanted. Life was good.

This professional medical society held a national conference every year, and that year the location was in San Francisco. I was too new of an employee to be considered for travel, but one of the older women took a liking to me and suggested that I ask. "What's the worst that could happen?" she asked. "They say 'no' and you don't go? You're already not going."

Ask and you shall receive. Words from the Bible that we can use every day. I believe people genuinely want to help, to give, to share. I did ask my supervisor about San Francisco. She gave it some thought and said yes. That trip was a life-changing experience, opening the door to a love of travel that hasn't closed. San Francisco is one of the world's great cities, and after registering conference participants from morning to noon, I had the rest of the day to explore the city's streets, gawk at drummers in Candlestick Park and join new friends for nighttime music concerts. All I had to do was ask.

I left that job for another, as lead secretary for a local hospital. I enjoyed the job, the people and the many experiences of hospital life. I worked in the Transportation Department, coordinating twenty male transporters who delivered patients to appointments, operations and, if things didn't go as planned, to the morgue.

I was the only Latina in a position of some responsibility and, being in my early twenties, felt invincible. However, I was also naive. I was not aware that some people looked at young women, young Latinas, as sex objects. At that time, sexual harassment had not come into our collective consciousness. Many breakrooms and some offices had nude pin-up calendars or *Playboy* foldouts displayed on the walls.

One particular hospital employee swaggered about the hospital with all the confidence of a young Dr. Kildare, although his position was that of nursing manager. He was handsome and personable. He was the first non-Latino male to engage me in a conversation. I felt important when he made it a point to seek me out. I took his interest in my work as a blessing. I found out differently when he asked me to meet him in his office for a break. I was more than shocked when in the middle of a conversation that had taken a more personal turn than I expected, he unzipped his pants, pulled out his penis and began to masturbate. This wasn't the only time I've experienced sexual harassment in a working environment or had a man expose himself to me, but this was the only time that I felt used. I thought this person wanted to help me advance professionally. I left his office and avoided him.

The encounter taught me a valuable lesson: Pay attention and learn to distinguish those who truly want to help you from those who want to take advantage of you. Listen. Paraphrasing the poet Maya Angelou, "People will tell you who they are. Just listen."

Another hospital employee, a very nice young man from Bogotá, Colombia, also took an interest in me. He was a full-time university student and worked full time at the hospital at night. He was shocked that I didn't speak Spanish well, and even more shocked that I wasn't in college. His family had sacrificed to send him to school in the United States, and here I was born and raised in this country, was smart and yet hadn't even thought of college. He encouraged me to apply to community college, suggesting that I could work as a transporter and attend school. There had never been a female transporter, and I was sure the supervisor would laugh at me.

But ask I did, and the supervisor said yes. And I did apply to the city college and was accepted. Soon, I was working the night shift as a transporter, taking bodies to the morgue, and going to college full-time.

Ask and you will receive. Four years later, after many twists and turns, this same advice would place me on my career path. After graduating with a BS degree in radio, television and film from the University of Texas, I followed my heart, which was attached to a radical Chicano graduate student, to the University of Michigan at Ann Arbor. I decided to continue my education and was accepted in the Communications Department graduate program. In the middle of this masters program, with the summer off, I returned to Chicago to spend time with my family and planned to volunteer at the local PBS station. The volunteer interview led to a job offer, which meant leaving the masters program—and the guy my heart was not so attached to anymore.

I had experienced the ups and downs of living with this older PhD candidate for five years. With our own personal baggage and our very strong personalities, we didn't fit in the house. He had introduced me to the world of higher education and encouraged me to think big, to challenge myself. Unfortunately, he was also working through his own issues that caused outbursts of anger that resulted in physical confrontations between us. I remembered my mom always fighting back, and so did I.

The job offer in Chicago provided the perfect excuse to take a few steps outside our life together, steps that soon led to the end of the relationship. We were together for a very important part of our lives, a crucial time in my young adulthood. It took some time to forgive each other. Today, however, we are friends.

Taking the step to return to Chicago led to doors opening I never dreamed existed.

I took the jump and accepted the job as associate producer for film critics Roger Ebert and Gene Siskel's movie review program, "At The Movies." It was—and still is—my all-time favorite job. I spent almost every day with two guys who knew everything about the movies. Every day we'd attended two or three movie screenings, and I listened as they discussed the movie's good and bad points. It was a dream job.

After two years, the producer left the show unexpectedly. As the associate producer, I knew I had to keep the show going —which I did and did well for the next three months.

Imagine my surprise when I heard the executive producer was arranging interviews to fill the producer position. It took all the courage I could muster to knock on her door and ask why I wasn't being considered for the position. She gave the very simple answer of, "You didn't ask." So I did, and was soon named producer of the show.

That show took on a whirlwind five-year tour of the television and movie businesses. I traveled with Siskel and Ebert to Las Vegas, selling the show to television executives. We attended movie premiere s and screenings in New York and Los Angeles. The show was nominated for two national Emmy Awards. I produced a number of documentaries with Roger, three of them at the Cannes International Film Festival. One of my fondest memories is celebrating my 30th birthday with a group of international filmmakers at a hillside restaurant in Provence, France, overlooking the Cote d'azur. All that happened because I knocked on a door and asked for what I wanted.

Ask. Always ask. Ask with confidence. Ask with a smile. Ask as if you know what you're doing and as if you know you have something great to offer. More than likely, you do!

Sometimes You Gotta Jump

I would venture to say that nine out of ten immigrants would much rather stay in their homeland. People leave their country, their family, their home because they can't survive there and want a better life for their family.

I had to leave my hometown and my family to reach for a dream. Twice. The first time led me to receive a quality education. The second time led me to Hollywood. My dream was to tell stories, stories that began in my heart, my community, my family and my circle of friends.

It was a very difficult decision to pack up my apartment, but my then-current love had already left Chicago for the bright lights of Hollywood. We were talking marriage, and I was financing his foray into "the business" by paying his living expenses. Little did I know that I was also financing his affair with a girl he had met in Los Angeles. To complicate matters and quell my sadness at being left behind, I had an affair with a man in Chicago. What an emotional mess.

Trying to make things work, I accepted a low-level production job in L.A. without even asking what it would pay. How bad could it possibly be? Turned out, I left a $60,000-a-year position for a job that paid $400 a week. I cried when I received my first paycheck.

It was the start of a long crying jag. I cried because within a few months of leaving my hometown, my father died. I felt that I had deserted my family, and yet, knew I couldn't return home. I cried because I discovered my boyfriend's affair with his agent's secretary, in the worst way: Polaroid photographs. I cried because I was sleeping on a friend's couch and had no idea how I was going to support myself. My life had become a "B" movie script.

I cried for weeks with this deep, crazy, confusing heartbreak. I screamed at the man I thought I was going to marry. I pleaded. I wrote letters reminding him of our commitment. He left notes on my door insisting that he loved me, wanting to try to make it work, then refused to speak with me for weeks. We were a whirlwind tornado of love and hate. ¡Un *remolino de mierda!* Finally, exhausted, we gave up. He was not coming back, and I didn't want him back. We were both too hurt, too tired, broken.

I remember the evening that I knew I had to accept the end of this relationship. Anita Baker on my audio cassette player singing, "Here me calling out your name. I feel no shame" over and over again. But I was ashamed. I had drank too many rum and Cokes, and couldn't stop crying. A new friend who I met working on a film production came over to help me get off the kitchen floor and into bed. Her words still make me smile, "You thought he was all that and a bag of chips, but he's just the crumbs."

It took a while, but I was able to jump out of the life circle I shared with that man and into a new one. It was a long jump, but I survived. New friends and show business professionals offered me assistance and encouragement. I worked hard and embraced my love of writing. This helped me discover my mission in life: To be a part of creating a realistic image of Latinos and Latinas in the movies and on television.

Because of this focus, I've worked on some of the most exciting projects that have elevated the Latino image, including "Selena," "My Family, *Mi Familia*," "American Family" and "Resurrection Blvd." I've co-written and co-produced an epic documentary on the image of Latinos in film, "The Bronze Screen: 100 Years of the Latino Image in Hollywood Cinema," and a profile documentary on the Mexican-American troubadour, Lalo Guerrero. When asked if I'm a writer or a Latino writer, I'm very proud to say, "I'm a Latina-Chicana-from-Chicago writer! ¿Y qué?"

Close the door to those who are hurting you, or those who don't value you. Jump out of any circle of friends, away from lovers, or even friends and family members who don't respect and love you. Jump into a life that *you* create, that you deserve. Just jump!

Love. You Get What You Believe You Deserve

My first serious boyfriend was a terrific guy from the hood. Although most of his friends were in gangs, he wasn't. I liked that about him. He could go to any party, hang out with any group, and still keep his autonomy. Everyone wanted to be his friend. That was because he was good at what he did: fixing cars. He always had a fun car to get around in, and he would repair your heap for a few bucks and a smile. He was handsome. He had goals.

We met during high school while both of us were going out with others. We went to my school prom, but not with each other. We spent much of the prom dance and the next-day picnic sending silent goo-goo-eyed messages to each other. I learned how seductive it could be to flirt with someone while in a relationship with someone else.

After the prom, I broke up with my then-boyfriend and started dating this young man. We were together for two years, when he quit college and joined the Chicago Police Department. This new combination, he a cop and me, a politicized college student, didn't work. I stayed in the relationship, but took up with someone new—on the side. I eventually did the same thing to the new guy. While in college living with the grad student, I had an affair with a student in my film production class. I'm not proud of these choices.

By my early thirties, I realized that I hadn't stayed true to any of my relationships. I didn't have whatever it took to make a clean break when that loving feeling was lost.

I went into counseling and began to unravel the complexities that kept me from fully committing to a relationship. Some of it was reminiscent of my father: the desire to have a good time and to return to a safe and loving home. Some of it was my mother's DNA: staying in a relationship, but refusing to accept any nonsense. I figured that if I had one foot in and one foot out of a relationship, I had the upper hand. The result was a catastrophic emotional mess in which I chose to love men who couldn't possibly ever commit to me, men who were fun loving, stimulating, dangerous and completely unable to make a commitment. A terrific psychologist helped me discover this about myself one cold, gray morning. She stated that I had been "dating my father," choosing to be in a relationship with men who wouldn't commit to me because I couldn't make a commitment. I couldn't commit or be faithful because I feared being hurt, being left behind. By trying to change these men, I was trying to "fix" what I thought was wrong with my dad, whom I loved with all my hear.

Now *that* was a revelation. And a mess.

It would take a number of years and a lot of work before I could say that I was ready for a true commitment with someone I would truly love and be faithful to. The road to this wonderful place took a clinical psychologist, three family counselors, a number of self-help books, a few self-help seminars, a couple of spiritual retreats and a real connection to Spirit, but I got there. After a few relationships gone sour and a lot of soul-searching, I was able to stand up, say *and* believe, "I deserve a good man to stand next to me and say that he loves me and is committed to me. I deserve this because I am a committed, one-man woman, ready to love with all my heart."

Our friends cannot give us the professional help we need to navigate the complicated emotional waters of our lives. If you need a good cry, call a friend. If you need solid guidance and advice on how to manage your life, get thee to a counselor!

Know that you deserve to be loved by a partner who loves and respects you. Believe that you love and respect your partner enough to be monogamous in body, mind and emotion. Realize and manifest what you deserve. I did—and that's when I met the true love of my life, my life partner and husband.

I did have to go out of my safety zone to meet him. I had been in an almost five-year relationship with a good guy who just happened not to believe in marriage. He told this to me from the get-go. He never lied to me or led me to believe otherwise; I just chose not to listen to him. He was perfect for the "scared me," the me who at my core was afraid of making a commitment and getting hurt. When I fixed that, I wanted to make a commitment and be committed to. It was a great turning point in my life to be able to ask for what I wanted—a committed relationship. That meant marriage. We parted as friends.

At that time, online dating was not as acceptable as it is today; it had a certain desperate quality about it. But the only men I was meeting as a work-at-home writer were the FedEx guy and the mailman. While I had a great life, filled with terrific friends, peace with my family, and doing what I loved to do professionally, I still felt it would be good to have a man in my life, one who was ready to love and be loved completely, without reservations.

I hit the jackpot on my first foray into computer dating. I asked for everything I wanted: intelligent, kind-hearted, Latino, with an interest in sports, music, travel, movies, books. Ready to love and be loved. And spiritual. The first name sent to me was the only man I met, dated, got engaged to and sixteen months later, married. I think St. Jude had something to do with it, too. And maybe St. Anthony, the saint you pray to when you've lost something. My beautiful *abuelita* had given me a prayer years and years ago, telling me, "Your husband is lost. St. Anthony will help you find him." Did I pray to St. Jude for this impossible request? Did I ask St. Anthony to help me find my one true love? I'll leave that up to you to decide.

I know in my heart, I received the best of what life and the universe had to offer, and then some—because I was ready to receive it. Everything that had happened up to that point in my life had prepared me to love and accept this great man into my heart and fully commit to him.

Love Yourself, Love Your Life

The worst morning I could ever imagine is waking up as an eighty-five-year-old wondering, "What would have happened if I had. . . ." Fill in the blanks. "If I had gone to college? If I had prayed? If I had respected myself? If I had truly, madly, deeply loved myself?" Maybe eighty-five years old shouldn't be the cut-off line. One of my elderly friends is ninety-two, and she's one of the best college students I've ever had the pleasure of teaching.

Perhaps she didn't want to wake up when she was eighty-six and ask, "What if?" She enrolled in college.

Ahhh . . . Loving Your Self. This is where the rubber meets the road. This is the grandmother of all self-help rules, and the one most of us have a difficult time understanding and following. This is the one I had the most trouble living. Love Your Self. It's probably difficult to achieve because it seems so nebulous, so tenuous. "How could I possibly not love myself?"

The easy answers: You do *not* love yourself if you are not taking care of your health, if you abuse alcohol, drugs, or food. You do not love yourself if you've chosen someone else's road instead of your own. You do not love yourself if you remain in any relationship where you are not valued. You'll know this is true if the quiet little voice in your head and heart, your conscience, your God, keeps reminding you.

The good news is that once you claim love for yourself, you'll never fall out of it. Never. Once you know self-love is a good thing, you'll love yourself unconditionally. That's not to say that you won't break up with yourself every now and then, and choose an experience that is not fulfilling or valuable to you. However, you'll soon realize what you have to courageously do to correct it, to make it matter to you.

Find a way to tune into you. Find a spirituality you can live with. Go to the ocean. Visit a forest. Sit quietly, meditate and listen. Five minutes of quiet thought can provide a wealth of advice from the one who loves you the most. You. Be responsible for your life. Respond to your life. Respond to your history. Respond to your choices, opportunities, your instincts. Be "Response Able."

Know that every experience, sacrifice, accomplishment, setback, good decision, bad decision, every love story or heartbreak has a reason and has placed you where you are today.

Truly loving yourself gives you the strength to create your own life, make your own decision and be able to say, "I love my life!" and mean it.

JOSEFINA LÓPEZ is the founding artistic director of CASA 0101 and is currently developing the musical version of her film *Real Women Have Curves*. She is a novelist, playwright, screenwriter, artist and bon vivant. Her first novel, *Hungry Woman in Paris* is in stores and online. Josefina is also the co-founder of Brooklyn & Boyle Literary & Artistic Salon.

www.JosefinaLopez.co
www.HungryWomaninParis.com

The Unlovable

I WAS BLONDE, HAZEL-EYED AND BEAUTIFUL BY AMERICAN standards. But by a woman's standards, I was cursed. I was drawn to bad boys, men who needed fixing, men who abused. In my search to find a man who would find me lovable, I lost myself and my innate power as a woman. I did find strength in my creativity, in my sexuality and in my heart, but I gave up my power every time I believed I was not good enough. It has been a journey to get back to my authentic self: a woman who is lovable in her own right. A woman who will never put up with a man's crap again....

That Perfect Man

Back in Mexico, when I was about three, I was up in a tree crying. My father climbed up to ask me what was wrong. He looked like Pedro Infante, a Mexican movie star, and I really thought he was Pedro because he had a guitar and boots—the whole cowboy outfit. I was in love with my father and thought he was perfect: my protector and the hero of the little movie in my mind. I told him I did not want him to leave. I made him promise me that he wouldn't, but he still left to *el norte*.

I felt as though I was not good enough to keep him. My father had to be in the United States to help support his eight children and couldn't return to Mexico every Christmas, as my mother, my siblings and I had hoped. He was undocumented and had to figure out a way to get back each time. One Christmas, I had expected to receive a doll because I had been good all year. When he did not come, I didn't understand. It seemed unfair that the neighbor's child, who had been a brat, was getting rewarded with toys. I was so disappointed, and I kept asking, "Why? Why?"

At that age, the only answer I could come up with was I was not "good enough." I was very close to my father. We used to play a lot together. The times he was able to return to Mexico he would whisk me up and down and call me "Locadia," crazy little one, and I would call him "Locadio." Finally, when I was five years old, my father was able to get enough money to bring my mother, my little sister and me to the United States. My older brothers and sisters would have to remain in Mexico until things were better financially.

I was so happy that at last I would have my father around me every day. I just wanted to make him happy and please him. I desperately wanted his approval and did whatever I could to get his attention. I took my mother for granted but put my father on a pedestal.

However, that perfect image came crashing to an end when I found out through my mother's crying that he was having an affair with the woman who was our tenant.

At the age of twelve, this devastating news planted yet another seed of self-hatred. What was so difficult and painful was the way I found out. My family lived with ten people in a two-bedroom house with only one bathroom, *ay!* My little sister and I slept in the living room on the sofa. The only phone in the house was in the living room.

One night, my mother got on that phone and started a conversation in whispers. When the news she was conveying got too painful, her voice got louder and her crying grew. I was awakened by her sobs. I pretended to sleep, but I heard everything. My life would never be the same.

"He's been picking her up at the park... I saw it with my own eyes," she whispered into the phone, not wanting anyone else to know. For many days afterwards, I woke up to my mother's crying. My chest felt tight and my gut hurt to know the truth. What was also painful was the fact that his mistress was my best friend's mother. I cried under my blankets, hoping my mother would not hear me. I cried because I had lost both my best friend and my father, and I could feel my mother's broken heart.

I wanted to talk to my mother about it, but I didn't know how. Would she deny it and tell me I was just dreaming or making it up? One day, right after playing outside, I came inside my house and walked to the bathroom. The door was slightly ajar, and I assumed it was empty so I walked in. My mother sat on top of the toilet, crying, looking distraught, without any hope. I asked what was wrong and she said, "Nothing."

My heart shrank, I felt helpless, felt my mother's pain in my chest and stomach. I couldn't believe my father could cause such heartache to my mother, to someone he loved. My father was the one having the affair, but it was my mother who was hiding, who was ashamed, keeping her secret. Her pain became mine.

I asked, "Is it my father?"

She didn't want to tell me.

I told her I had overheard her conversations on the phone, and she nodded, not denying it anymore. I could tell she didn't know what to do.

My mother said, "Ni modo," the universal anthem of the helpless. That was my mother's usual statement that would temporarily solve everything.

I felt sorry for her and wanted so badly to provide an answer. "There is no way." In my mind, I had to find a way to give my mother some hope. At that age, I didn't realize what a difficult situation she was in: the mother of eight children, most of whom were undocumented, with no means of supporting herself. I could not accept this situation. Even though I was only twelve, I knew something was terribly wrong with that scenario.

Why did women have to put up with this? I promised my mother I was going to do something so that someday women felt like they had a choice, so they could walk away from men who hurt them and choose a life where they were in charge of their destiny.

My mother listened, trying to smile. I wanted to make her smile. I wanted to take away her pain and rescue her. I told her I wanted to start a revolution so that women didn't have to suffer. My mother smiled with some light in her eyes, impressed by my determination.

Taking a Stand

My mother finally stood up to my father a few weeks later, when the affair was practically in her face. She had forbidden me to visit my best friend and had even kicked her out of our house in my presence. I would still sneak over to her house and play with her until her mother called her in.

One day, my father came home with a bag full of brassieres he had found in a garbage dumpster where he worked. I was so delighted because I was just getting breasts and most of the bras were so small. My father told us that they were probably stolen and maybe had been dumped there to get rid of excessive merchandise, so we should keep quiet about the find.

I couldn't wait to tell my best friend, who already had breasts.

I went to her house to brag that I had so many bras. She shared with me that her mother also came home with a bag full of bras for her and her sisters. We compared the straps on our bras and realized they were the same brand. I was so jealous and couldn't believe what it really meant. My best friend was clueless and didn't make the connection that her mother was having an affair with my father. I couldn't tell her because she had already suffered enough—her estranged father was an alcoholic who beat them and her mother.

I ran home and told my mother. She became furious at my father. She had suspected he was giving his mistress money. Now, she was disgusted that he had given his mistress first choice at the bras and had given us the leftovers. I was also deeply hurt at the thought that my father preferred his mistress and her eight children to us. I felt that perhaps he didn't love us because we weren't good enough for him.

My mother confronted him with the bag of brassieres. Evidence. My father did not deny it. He couldn't.

"Every man sooner or later does it," he said without apology.

My sisters got angry when they discovered the news and yelled obscenities at him, criticizing him as a "macho" as they left the house. It was a family spectacle, a painful scene from one of the many *telenovelas* my mother was addicted to.

I also left the house with my sisters. We went to the garage. I carried a plate of boiled corn and stuffed myself with a corn on the cob. I cried into my corn, mixing the butter with my tears. When I finished, I went around the house, peeked through a window and saw the fight. My mother announced that she was going to go over to his mistress' house to confront her in front of her children so that they would know what a "whore" she was. She made for the door. My father stepped in front of her so she couldn't pass. My mother slapped his face, pushed and pulled, but he would not move.

It was violent and ugly, but I preferred to see my mother like this than the defeated woman on the toilet.

Days after their fight, my mother got a job as a seamstress and gained some financial independence from my father. She demanded that he hand over his check to her every week and declared that she would manage the money. I begged my mother to divorce him, but she didn't. It's clear even today that she will never leave him.

I never wanted a relationship like that.

I remember thinking that I wanted to get an education so badly so that I could support myself and leave a man if I ever I needed to. I was never going to be dependent on a man and put up with his abuse. I began to hate my father. I couldn't stand to look at him or take orders from him because I had lost all respect for him. I told my mother that I hated him, and she said I couldn't, that no matter what he had done, he was still my father. I buried my anger and swallowed my pain.

The Curse

Coming from a family of eight children, there was a lot of pain to go around but not a lot of love, it seemed. My parents kept us alive, they fed us, put clothes on our back, sheltered us and tried to keep us safe, but they never said, "I love you." Had we grown up in Mexico it would have been a given that they loved us, but we grew up in the U.S. watching TV in which white people on the *Brady Bunch* said they loved each other all the time. I assumed that my parents didn't love me because they never said it. I grew up hungry for affection, wanting to hear any words of encouragement and love. (Years later, I realized that my parents didn't know how to say beautiful loving words to us because they never got those words from their own parents.) When my mother, the youngest of nine, was two years old, she was given away to her sister because her mother was tired of taking care of children. My mother felt like an orphan, with no self-esteem. My father was treated like a servant child and was exploited, even up until he was an adult, when he finally broke away from his parents to go to *el norte*. Both parents had no education, no self-esteem or knowledge of how to transmit their love with words or affection. (This is something they still work on in their own relationship today).

I wanted someone desperately to show me they cared about me, but I was always cautious about my reputation as a good girl and never pursued attention from boys. Although my parents hated the Catholic Church for punishing them for their indiscretions (my mother eloped with my father, a married man, and lived out of wedlock with six "bastard" children), they still very much upheld Catholic beliefs concerning the role of women. It was spelled out that sex was only for married people and that my father would not tolerate a daughter of his getting pregnant out of wedlock, which was precisely his and my mother's history. We were not allowed to date, yet we could not leave the house until we were married, which meant we had to sneak around with our boyfriends. A man had to ask him for our hand in marriage; otherwise, he insisted there could be no men in our lives. Two of my sisters got married just to get out of the house, only to end up with husbands just as controlling as my father.

At fifteen, I had my first kiss, my first boyfriend and my first betrayal. He broke my heart. His betrayal only confirmed that I was unlovable and that men would just leave me. Soon after that, I entered my first depression. I would use food and relationships to self-medicate and get me through the hard times.

Often I obsessed over a particular boy to make my sad and boring life meaningful. Growing up undocumented and a girl in a Mexican household made it clear to me that my life was worthless. I was there to be of service to a man and should consider myself lucky if he didn't beat me or cheat on me. I very much swore I would not end up marrying a Latino man who believed those things. Instead, I would marry a man who was my partner—not my master and owner. I told this to my father one night when he criticized my mother for being dirty. He criticized her so much that just to spite him my mother gave up caring about how messy. My father told me I needed to learn to clean and cook, otherwise no man would want to marry me. I think I replied, "Well, I'm not going to marry a macho, I'm going to marry a modern man."

"Well, you're going to have to support him," he countered.

"I'd rather support him than have him criticize me all the time and treat me like his servant."

"What man would want to marry you?" he spit out, like a dagger to my heart.

I probably imagined that he said this, but it has echoed in my mind so much that it feels like it was the truth. He cursed me, I felt.

Some man would want to marry me. I was sure of it. I set out to prove to him wrong.

The Hunger

When I was eighteen, I learned what love was. At my arts high school, I had met a boy named Daniel, who was Anglo and very mature for his age. He was socially awkward and not very attractive, but was extremely intelligent and witty. We came from such different worlds. His parents both had gone to college, he was an only child and he was tired of his parents always telling him how much they loved him and how proud they were of him.

I felt like no one wanted me. My mother had confessed to me that after having three children, she wanted to stop, but she had no say over her fertility. She hated sex and the fact that children were imposed on her. I didn't blame her or hate her for feeling that way, but it made me feel like I was not wanted and should never have been born. There were times when I actually wished I could have died to be one less burden on my poor mother. There were times when I considered ending my life to end the pain of feeling like a waste of a life. Years later, when studies came out about how teenage Latinas have the highest suicide rate, I would realize that I was not alone.

Daniel and I fell in love because, although he was deeply loved and appreciated by his parents, he felt like he was a disappointment to them. We commiserated and even shared something special. When I had my first sexual experience I wanted it to be an expression of me and not just a spontaneous act of lust—or worse—an act of "love," the only justification some women give themselves for having sex and liking it.

The first time would have to be an act of reclaiming my right to my body, my sexuality and an affirmation for me having sex. Daniel and I had discussed losing our virginity and at first had agreed not to do it. I actually spent lot of time debating whether I would have sex before marriage. The message all along had been clear: if I had sex before marriage, I was "ruined," as though I was an object that was tampered with, like someone breaking the seal on a bottle of aspirin and opening it.

After our discussions, I finally realized, "I am a human being, damn it! I have worth, I have a mind, I have ideas and dreams." What is that worth? My virginity is only one aspect of who I am, and sex can be a natural expression of connection and self-love.

Then one night when I was over at his house, his parents called saying they were stuck on the road and were not going to be home for a while. We seized the opportunity. It happened naturally and beautifully. We were both nervous, but excited to be initiated into adulthood. We took all the precautions and, afterwards, we hugged. We cherished our experience. When my mother had described sex to me, she had almost described it as rape. But mine had been a beautiful experience that made me feel like I had reclaimed a part of my humanity instead of losing a part of myself.

Our relationship lasted until the end of senior year, when he had to go away for the summer. When he returned from vacation, he broke up with me because he said I was too needy and he felt helpless, unable to rescue me from my painful situation at home and in my life. I felt pretty bad about myself, knowing that he was telling me the truth. I was running away from myself and was giving someone else the responsibility to love me.

"It's not that you want me as your boyfriend, it's that you need to have a boyfriend," I recalled him saying. I walked around with my heart on my sleeve, wanting to hand it to someone else to take care of because it was too painful to do it for myself. If I had to take care of my own heart, then that truly meant nobody loved me. Years later, I would learn that the opposite was true, but confronting that truth at nineteen was not yet possible.

I made the mistake of not believing the relationship was over and constantly called Daniel, hoping he would take me back. I would settle for any attention he would give me; it was still better than being alone with my suicidal thoughts. I would go over to his house and do whatever I could to get him to have sex with me so that I could get some affection that way. It worked, but it didn't have the positive effect I had hoped for. We would have sex in the dark and after I got what I wanted—a man to touch and caress me—I would cry because I felt pathetic resorting to that. I cried, hoping he would stop humping me and genuinely show me that he cared. He never did.

On the bus ride home, I felt sorry for myself: I was the most unlovable person on the planet. When I think of this now, I just want to go hug that nineteen-year-old Josefina and tell her that everything was going to turn out all right, that it was not her fault her parents didn't know any better, and that all human beings deserve and need love and affection.

I continued to hang out with Daniel, thinking I had reconquered his heart, but once after sex, he shared that even though he still cared about me, he never saw himself married to me. It came as more than a painful shock; it was like acid on my face. He told me that the person he would marry would have to love music and play an instrument.

What? My parents had no money for music lessons. I felt sorry for myself. I wish he would have just told me, "I can't marry you because you're not white." I would have understood, could even justify it, but saying I couldn't play an instrument made me ashamed of being poor and untalented in that area. This was more evidence against me to prove that my father was right: No man would want to marry me.

Long Distance Nightmares

Several months later, I started dating Gabriel, the ex-president of MEChA, who schooled me on what it meant to be a Chicano. I can truly say he opened my eyes and helped me gain a Chicana/o conscience. He was a pre-med student who wanted to give back to his community. I was so impressed by his desire for equality for all and his sincere attempt at being a modern man.

However, I soon discovered he had a "virgin/whore" complex and had to be retrained to expand his mind concerning sex. I have found that Latino men compartmentalize women into "virgins"—women they want to marry—and "whores"—women they just want to mess around with. It's a lot of Catholic B.S. fed to them by their mothers and their own egos, supporting the belief that women are there merely to fulfill roles of servitude to men. With the exception of one guy, I've had to reeducate all my boyfriends concerning sex with a real woman versus a porno or imaginary woman. They had to expand their minds, read books, go to therapy, if they wanted to continue being with me.

Gabriel and I dated for a year before we got serious and had to decide where our paths were taking us. I was accepted to UCLA film school for undergraduate studies, something I'd always wanted to do. Though he had applied to UCLA's medical school, he had not been accepted. He headed for med school in Chicago.

He was angry with me and couldn't believe I wasn't going with him. I debated with myself and after a while, decided that I would rather go with him and discover he wasn't the man of my dreams than not go with him and discover he was the man of my dreams and regret it the rest of my life. I followed on the condition he would marry me after the first year of medical school. He agreed.

Like a love-struck idiot, I went to Chicago to freeze my ass off and discover the hardships of dating a medical student. Luckily, I found Columbia College Chicago and got to thrive as an artist, even though my love life was a struggle. After a year of medical school, Gabriel came up with excuses on why he could not marry me. By then I was in too deep to just leave. I waited another year. When he didn't propose, I moved back to L.A. to begin my screenwriting career on a high-paying sitcom.

With men, I learned, you have to give them an ultimatum. They propose or you walk. If they love you, they will propose. If they don't, they did you a favor. If they are cowards—they really love you but won't propose—leave. After a few months, they'll come begging you to take them back.

So Gabriel came back when he realized how much he loved me and he proposed. We got married in Las Vegas at the Graceland chapel in a Spanish ceremony with no family or friends. We wanted to keep it a secret. This was our commitment to endure a long distance marriage. The first months were easy and after four months, we realized we needed to be together. He took time off from medical school and came to live with me in L.A. I was busy writing on a Chicano sketch comedy show and was also getting acting roles, which my manager encouraged me to take.

Gabriel was annoyed that he had taken time off to be with me and here I was busy with my career. I guess he probably felt the way I did when I was back in Chicago. I had been keeping him abreast of my schedule and invited him to come down to the studio to watch me work and act. One night I told him I would probably be home late. He said he preferred to stay home and wait. When I arrived, he refused to talk to me. (I look back now and wonder how I could have fallen in love with a jealous man like him, who shut down when he felt any strong feelings. Oh, yeah—my father did that. I would uncover that pattern a few boyfriends and husbands later).

When I asked him what was wrong, all he said was, "You know."

I tried getting him to talk and then he exploded. We started screaming, and I knew then that this marriage was not going to work. When he left for Chicago after the holidays, I knew I had to end it but wasn't sure how to do it.

My family, who did not know we had already gotten married in Vegas, was excited about me getting married in Los Angeles a few months later. I couldn't go through with it. I called it off. Gabriel hated me after that and made it impossible to get a divorce.

I told my mother I had ended the relationship and expected her to tell me I was crazy, but instead she was compassionate. She had watched an episode of *Cristina*, a Spanish talk show, about divorced women who preferred to be single than put up with men's crap.

"I guess we brought you to this country so that you wouldn't have to put up with crap like I did."

I couldn't believe what I was hearing. I was so happy my mother understood, that I decided to take her to Italy with me, the place where I was to have had our dream honeymoon.

The Vision

A few weeks before the trip, I was walking around the Gaslamp Quarter in San Diego, depressed and lonely. Even though I had obtained success by having my play, *Real Women Have Curves*, produced simultaneously in San Diego and Dallas, I still felt empty and completely alone. I missed Gabriel.

That's what sucks about having your best friend be your boyfriend. I walked into a café, saw a tarot card reader and sat at her table. Like a typical client who goes to a reader, I confessed that I felt completely alone and wanted to find a soul mate.

"Don't feel alone. Your soul mate misses you, too, and he will find you this year." She said I didn't have to do anything because he would find me. "He's Asian, he's tall and he has reddish hair," she added.

My heart lit up, and I got so excited knowing that there was somebody for me, that I wasn't alone in the world. When I was growing up, my mother was pretty psychic—yes, the first time my father cheated on her she didn't know, but after that she would always know with whom he was going to cheat before he even knew. (I also have this psychic gift.) Coincidences, signs, angels and premonitions were something I never questioned, because through my creative writing I was open to all sorts of divine assistance.

Before I left to Italy, I saw the tarot card reader a few more times. I told her that I had wanted to go to Rome since I was twelve and didn't know why I was going, but my heart and gut kept telling me I had to go.

"Stay close to your mother and, if you meet someone, don't sleep with him. Take his contact information and write to him instead," she advised me.

With my mother and my video camera, we flew from L.A. to Rome, stopping in Milan to refuel. As we walked to the gate, I saw a tall, thin Chinese man with reddish hair. He wore striped pants and cool clothes. He was busy reading an Asian newspaper.

Is that the man who is supposed to fall in love with me, I wondered? Why isn't he looking at me, I thought? I sat behind him, hoping he would notice me, but he wouldn't turn to look at me. I told my mother how unusual it was to see an Asian man by himself in Italy. I wondered what he was doing in Europe. I got distracted and when I looked back at his seat, he was gone. I felt dejected. I would never get to know him and what he was doing in Italy. A few minutes later, my mother and I re-boarded the plane. He was sitting in my seat. I smiled, loving this coincidence. Since there were empty seats available, I just sat in the next seat over.

I wanted to talk to him but was convinced he didn't speak English. He looked so foreign that I didn't dare talk to him, yet I was fascinated by him. After a few minutes of translating for my mother from English to Spanish, I gained the confidence to try out my limited Italian. I found a map in an airline magazine and showed it to him.

"Where are you from?" I asked him in Italian.

He pointed to Japan. I was wrong. Then he asked me where I was from.

I told him Los Angeles.

He was excited to learn that. He introduced himself as Daisuke. I introduced myself but had to explain that I was Mexican American—and that's why I didn't have an American-sounding name.

We quickly uncovered that he was a director and I was a writer. We couldn't believe it.

I asked for his phone number in case I got lost in Rome. He suggested lunch the next day. Even though I hardly spoke Italian, we both made a great deal of effort to understand one another. We agreed to meet by his apartment near the Vatican. My mother had long ago yearned to visit the Vatican and was excited to finally get there. Daisuke became our guide and was so skilled in camera work, that he became our cinematographer.

By the time we all came out of the Vatican, Daisuke and I knew we loved each other. He seemed so familiar to me, and I couldn't believe we were managing to understand one another. By the end of the night I knew he would tell me he loved . . . As I write this, I find it so painful to continue.

That day was magical and to know how it ends stops me from going on, but I will be brief so as not to stir up the dragons and the drama of losing a part of my soul.

At the end of the night I went to the Coliseum with him. We held hands. There was a full moon and the setting was straight out of a movie. He asked if he could kiss me and I told him yes. It was a beautiful kiss and I couldn't believe how it all transpired. Yet, it was déjà-vu. After he kissed me, I knew he would say he loved me—and he did.

Then I snapped out of it, feeling like I was on Candid Camera or a victim of a reality show prank. I immediately shot back at him, "How can you possibly say you love me when you've only known me for one day?"

He replied, "In Japan, we believe that when people meet for the first time, their spirits can fall in love."

I melted when he said that, because I knew my soul connected with him, too. This was not about physical attraction, but something profound. I hesitated to tell him I loved him because I was afraid it was this man's M.O. with American women. As we danced under the moonlight, with the full moon bearing witness to this magical moment, I realized he was really baring his heart and soul to me. He was courageous enough to express what I was feeling, but in Italian it sounded even more beautiful and profound.

"*Io sono solo in questo mondo.*" I am alone in this world. "Do you need me?" he continued in Italian.

He wanted to make love to me because he was leaving for Spain the next morning and I was leaving for Florence. I told him I didn't want to get involved with him because I had already been in a long distance relationship and didn't want to go through the pain again. We walked back to my hotel and exchanged contact information, as I had promised the tarot card reader.

We wrote faxes and letters to one another for a year and a half. Our hearts grew fonder. Perhaps if email had existed back then, things would not have ended so painfully, but better to have loved and lost. I was convinced we were going to get married and he was going to move to Los Angeles with me. I even studied the Japanese language and Japanese civilization and culture. But destiny had other plans for us.

After waiting for him to call to let me know if he was coming to Los Angeles for Christmas, I gave up and called the whole thing off. It was painful, putting my life on hold. Here I was having another long distance relationship. That was too much for my aching heart. When I think about this part of my life, I still cry. I cry because we loved each other so much, yet love did not conquer all, and it was not enough to bring us together. I thought God had wanted us to meet to be together. I thought he was my reward for all the pain I had already gone through. After many months of not being together, I decided to fly to Japan to try to win him back and see if he would come to Los Angeles with me. I would prefer to hear that it was impossible directly from him so I could truly move on, rather than not know it and always be wondering what could have been. When I arrived in Japan, I saw an entirely different person.

In Italy, Daisuke had been so different. He had acted as though he were Italian, with a more loving, carefree manner. In Japan, he was all about work and was surprisingly stoic and cold. I managed to get him to open up to me.

He finally confessed that, at first, his father had given him his blessing to go to Los Angeles, but later begged him not to since he was the only living relative. It was his duty to stay and care for his sick father, who was in a convalescent home. I understood why he had to stay in Japan, but the truth didn't make it any less painful. I was willing to settle for a long distance relationship, but now it was he who did not want to go through that pain and frustration.

I asked, "Do you need me?"

He shook his head and said that he couldn't go on.

I wanted to make love to him, but he kept saying he had to get back to work. It was midnight and he had to get back to work.

He was a slave to his company. I felt sorry for him and the many Japanese people who had to work sixteen to eighteen hours a day. Then I realized that I, too, was a slave to my work.

When I returned to Los Angeles, my heart was devastated. I honestly didn't want to live. I believed that without this man, without his love, I had no reason to live. I became depressed. It all sounds very dramatic recalling this, but it was true. The one man I loved—not just with my heart, but with my very soul—did not want to love me anymore.

This was the ultimate confirmation that I was unlovable.

Years later, I went to see a healer who told me that indeed Daisuke was a twin soul, someone just like me, living a parallel existence in another part of the world. Also, in a past life in which I had been a gypsy in Spain in the 1600s, he had been my brother. When we saw each other in Italy, our souls had recognized each other, but our destiny would not be to spend our lives together. We were simply there to remind each other that we were not alone.

I really believed that we were meant to end up together, that because I had been such a good person my whole life, I somehow deserved to end up with him. It was not to be.

The Unlovable

I sought healing. I even joined an Asian men's support group to overcome the pain and sadness. It partly worked, but my soul still ached. I wanted so desperately to be loved. Why couldn't somebody love me? This wound continued to remind me of the original wound: the belief that I was unlovable and if my father couldn't love me, then why would I expect any man would?

The relationships that followed were more desperate attempts to be loved by anybody. I would shrink and make myself adaptable to the man I was with. I would love their music and make myself into the perfect girlfriend, only to discover later they were using me just for sex and wouldn't even consider me their girlfriend.

One time, I discovered I was dating a high-functioning sociopath, when a psychiatrist came to talk to our writing class about mental disorders and personality traits. Indeed, the person I thought was my boyfriend was someone who could not love. He hadn't bonded with his mother and could not commit to a person, and, oh my God, I finally had a breakthrough when a voice inside me asked, "Who am I being that I want so desperately to be loved by a man who cannot love me?"

That's when it struck me. I was attracted to men who did not want me. This was my game: I wanted to make these men fall in love with me because if I could convince them to love me, then it meant I was lovable. Instead, when I couldn't get them to love me, it reinforced the idea that I was unlovable. I won. I won by losing myself.

Then I remembered that there were, in fact, men who had been interested in me and expressed their love for me all along. I just thought they had been dumb.

The subconscious mind has a mind of its own. I thought they were dumb because they couldn't tell how unlovable I was. Yes, it makes no sense, but to the subconscious mind, which really runs the show, it did.

I went looking for the man who had sworn his love for me. Before I knew it, I was in bed with him and his manic depression. Sex was great with him. I felt very free having sex at this point in my life. He was such a generous lover who did not need to be educated—he was even more anxious to please me. This athletic man had stamina and could make love for hours, but sex alone could not keep me from seeing that we were wrong for one another. By the time I tried to get out, the relationship was beyond comprehension; it was beyond weird.

Let me just start by saying that if a man ever tries to convince you that he has a female stalker, unless he is a famous actor or rock star, you should run in the other direction or you're going to end up in therapy. This guy believed things like that. I stayed too long, way past the point of normal and had to get out fast.

I discovered that I might have been unlovable, but meeting someone even more broken, who needed stronger medication than me, might have meant, perhaps, life was not so hard after all. I wanted to be loved by someone, but being smothered was the other extreme. I started to see how it felt for some of my boyfriends when they were with me.

Ever since I wanted to prove my father wrong, I unconsciously never wasted my time dating. I just picked a man to obsess over and made him my boyfriend. I was interested or I was not. Unlike my best friend, who would go out with any man with a phone number, I was picky. I mostly picked broken men to the tango of drama: "I work out my issues with my father; you work out your issues with your mother."

My next victim—I say victim because as much as I wanted to love him, I simply used him to satisfy my need to be loved—was just as neurotic, but undiagnosed. Let's call him Steve, because I'm sure he is a better man now and would rather be called Steve than asshole or coward.

So I ran away from the last delusional boyfriend into the arms of another man who resented his father for being brilliant. This, I discovered a few months into the relationship, and found myself shrinking and being so small I didn't cast a shadow on him. I began to apologize for my creativity and, before I knew it, I would do anything to be with him, including denying my voice and my creative abilities. I am still embarrassed that I stayed with this man almost a year, when I clearly knew I should not have been around him at all.

At that time in my life, I was completely broke in every way. I had given up on my writing career after Daisuke. I couldn't get a job anywhere. My only experience up until then was writing TV pilots. I was completely dependent on Steve. He supported me, and I was ashamed that I could not financially contribute to our relationship. I had put myself in the situation I had sworn never to be in—completely dependent on a man.

I was also depressed and unstable, feeling like an orphan with no emotional support. My parents had already retired and moved back to Mexico. Most of my siblings, except for my youngest brother, were married with their own families. I had honestly thought I would never marry, but still wanted to prove to myself and my parents that I was lovable. I unconsciously sabotaged myself. I was a yo-yo: I wanted to get married; I didn't want to be married.

I was out of alignment with my true self.

Although I was unemployed, I had earned a reputation as an accomplished playwright and poet and had many fans and stories written about me in national magazines and newspapers. Steve wanted to break up with me because he didn't want to be known as my boyfriend and be left in my shadow. I should have broken up with him, but he finally did it first. I could not cling anymore.

I was embarrassed and ashamed to have to go live in my brother's garage, but I did. Unfortunately, I did not stay away from Steve. We still worked together on some programs for Latino filmmakers. After one of the workshops, he was furious at me because he had coordinated the event, yet the person teaching the workshop liked me better and thanked me for my work. In Steve's eyes, I was evil and manipulative. He hated me for again stealing his thunder.

I had forgiven and excused his abusive behavior because I understood his pain, his misfortunes, and didn't want to lose him. I had preferred to lose my self-respect than to lose him. Once, in a parking lot at a university campus, he began shouting insulting words at me. I told him to stop and he wouldn't, so I walked away. After I got in my car, I quickly went back to him because I did not want us to leave in anger. He was already in his car when I did something stupid: I grabbed his windshield wiper hoping he would stop. He didn't. As he backed out, the windshield wiper came off and tore the skin on the top of one of my fingers. I peeled off the skin and swiped my finger on his windshield, smearing the blood. He freaked out and took off.

A few minutes later, he returned with a vengeance.

I sat in my car crying when Steve drove up behind my car, got out and kicked in the taillight. He didn't kick it just once; he kicked it many times and then drove off. I couldn't believe he had done that or what else he might be capable of doing. I tried to start my car, but the battery was dead. Minutes later, Steve returned; I thought maybe to apologize. He ran toward me. I immediately tried shutting the door and locking my car, but he had already grabbed the handle and was stronger than I was. He grabbed my keys. I tried pulling them away. We played tug-of-war until he ripped them out of my hands. He took our old apartment keys away from me and tossed the rest of my keys across the parking lot. He drove off. I cried and walked across the lot to get my keys. By now there were onlookers. I was so embarrassed to be in that situation. I hurried back to my car and cried. My face was completely red from crying so much.

To make things worse, campus police showed up. They asked me what had happened, and I explained.

"Do you want to press charges?" one of the officers asked.

I immediately said no. Even though Steve had just done this, I still wanted to protect Steve. I understood why he felt like a loser and why he did what he did. I was so ashamed. I had read and knew so much about domestic violence, and yet, I did not want to press charges. I didn't want anyone to know about this; I just wanted to forget all of it.

"Are you sure?" the officer pressed on. "Your face is red. Did he punch you there?" He pointed to my cheekbone.

One time, Steve had punched me on the arm while I was driving. I had told him his so-called friend was not really his friend. I guess he must have heard that he was unlovable. I slapped him back, broke his glasses and yelled, "How dare you hit me while I'm driving!"

I knew that minute the relationship was over, but there I was, months later, with the hope that we could make it work.

"No, he didn't hit me. I've just been crying a lot. I can't believe what he did."

"Well, if you still want to press charges later, you can," the officer informed me.

They jump-started my car. I went home and cried on my bed until my brother knocked on my door to tell me I had a phone call.

It was Steve. I was shocked to discover he had gone to the police station by my house to place a report against me. He said he was scared of me, scared that I could retaliate and hurt him.

My jaw dropped and I wanted to laugh. I had just refused to press charges against him, and he had reported *me* to the police as though he were the victim. I felt so sorry for him because his version of reality was even more distorted than mine. It was clear to me this man was a coward. I considered myself lucky that it was over. I hung up on him and went back to my bed to wake up from that stupid nightmare.

True Love: A Man Loving You Loving Yourself

I could not get past my sentence that I was unlovable. I had read so many self-esteem books and had taken lots of workshops and seminars on self-love, I knew better. "Unlovable" was something so ingrained and cemented in my unconscious mind that I kept finding myself in situations where I kept quiet about my needs and hid my true self.

My true self is an authentic person who is brilliant and aspires to develop her genius and express herself in every artistic way possible. The woman I presented to a man was a "confident" and fun woman who made her boyfriend a priority and who didn't express her need to be the best she could be, even if that meant outshining the person she loved.

The pattern continued. I've been married a couple of times and will skip ahead to my last marriage, since by now you probably understand my M.O.

When I finally met Emmanuel, my current husband, I was in another depression and my finances were again in shambles. I was so lost that I wanted to be rescued once again. I went from being a feminist Amazon warrior to Cinderella so many times that I felt like I had multiple personalities. Emmanuel was my knight in shining armor who would sweep me away to a better life—I hoped. I willingly handed over the reins of my life and said, "Here, you be in charge. I can't take care of myself."

Emmanuel began as a loving boyfriend who slowly revealed his fangs and violent temper. I kept trying to run away from him and would always go back to him. He became controlling. When I gave birth to our first son, he became unbearable, even going so far as to tell me how to breastfeed. The "unlovable" doubts crept in. Did he care more about our son than me?

I consulted many people for help, including one spiritual counselor who told me, "You never fully commit to the men in your relationships because you are afraid you will be mistreated. They know you aren't fully committed. The men feel like they're not good enough for you and they resent you for it, proceed to mistreat you, and then you have your reasons to run away," he revealed to me.

I thought about how true this was for Steve and the string of other destructive boyfriends.

"This was something that was set in place back when you were young. Something you learned from your parents' relationship," he continued.

I took in his words and knew he was right.

"At the beginning of your relationships, you don't truly let a man see who you really are, so they fall in love with someone who is not truly you. Then when you finally want to reveal your true self to them, they don't want to see it because they can no longer be your rescuer. You don't own your power and when you want to take it back, they don't want you to be so powerful because it scares them. True love is a man loving you loving yourself."

I took his advice and tried being my true self, but Emmanuel was used to me agreeing with him and was set on how a family had to be and act. I fought him and myself until I took inventory of my life. Had I not tried to prove my father wrong and tried desperately to win my parents' approval, I might never have married him or had kids.

Back when I was married the first time, I spoke to my father after I had completed a communication seminar about our relationship. My interpretation of what he did made me resent him, but I didn't see the truth about him. He had the affair because he was tempted. It had nothing to do with *my* self-worth. I was the one who interpreted that I was unlovable and that he didn't love me because he left. I was the one who interpreted that I wasn't good enough because he had an affair.

I apologized to my father, and then he apologized to me. I had always wanted to hear that he loved me, but realized I had never said it to him.

I told him I loved him. He was sorry that he had never said he loved me. He felt that because he didn't have an education or any formal training, that he just wasn't good with words, but that he had always loved me.

I began to cry, feeling the wasted time trying to get that love from other men.

My father clarified that when he said no man would want to marry me, he had not meant that I was not worth marrying. He knew that very few men would be able to be with a woman who wanted so much freedom—and live the life she wanted to live. He actually came from a good place when he said it.

I confessed to Emmanuel that I didn't know if I wanted to be married because the kind of marriage and family he wanted was not what I wanted. We argued over so many things. A lot of the things he wanted, I felt, were the things he didn't get when he was growing up. He wanted to compensate for them through our marriage. I also felt completely taken for granted. He didn't understand that he needed to tend to our relationship first.

He didn't understand what I meant until I left.

Leaving Ghosts Behind

When I visited my children, Emmanuel told me he would do everything he could to win me back. I ignored him and tolerated his attempts at romancing me.

"Why didn't you do that when we were married? Why didn't you cherish me when you had the chance?" I yelled at him, full of anger and resentment so he would leave me alone.

I was finally seeing my self-worth and would not allow myself to be treated badly again.

It was a painful time. My older son cried and begged me, "Please don't go." It made my heart shiver. I remembered begging my father not to go to *el norte*. I felt like such a jerk, telling him I had to go. I left without looking back.

I wondered if this was the moment that would make my son interpret that he, too, was unlovable.

During this time I saw a therapist who hypnotized me to help me release all the anger I had for Emmanuel. In one of the sessions I was able visualize giving my mother a box full of her "shoulds" that I pulled out of my uterus. Many years before, a spiritual healer told me that I was on my way to getting cancer of the uterus if I didn't stop trying to be the perfect daughter. If I continued to resent Emmanuel and myself, I could eventually get cancer of the uterus, anyway. I also knew that I had certain limiting beliefs that would ensure I could not be creator. It felt great to give my mother back her garbage bag full of shoulds

—about what a Latina woman should be—that I'm certain were passed onto her by her mother, other women and the Catholic Church.

After many sessions, I forgave myself and my husband. I saw clarity concerning marriage and freedom. I chose to be married. I could work things out with my husband. After he committed to going to therapy, anger management therapy and leadership classes, I took him back. Having done many of these workshops myself, I knew they were not classes that were meant to fix him, but to give him the tools to become a man and find his life's purpose, too. My children were worth the effort. My self-esteem was worth the effort.

Clarity and Forgiveness from My Authentic Self

Forgiving is the key out of the gates of hell. In meditation, I often say I forgive all these men and ask that I be forgiven for all the pain I caused them, too. I know that I was not the poor victim. I know that in not coming from authenticity, that I, too, hurt them, even though I was doing the best I could at that time.

I love my life, and even though I feel like I have put myself through a lot of pain, there were a lot of gains and lessons to be learned. When I think of all the men in my life, I am now glad I went through it all because they taught me to value myself, love myself and own my power. I kept giving my power away. Now I truly have the life of my dreams because I realized that as a woman I have always been powerful.

I accepted my power when:
- I *believed* I was powerful.
- I believed I had the final word on my body; that included my sexuality, my fertility and the way I look.
- I did not accept someone else's notion of what it meant to be successful.

- I wanted the love of myself more than the love of my mother and my family.
- I understood that loving a man meant taking care of my needs and loving myself first—never compromising my dignity.
- I stopped believing that self-confidence was only for women who were thin, rich and perfect—and that I couldn't be loved and love myself until I had those three things.
- I heard my inner voice—my higher self—say I deserved more.
- I accepted that I'm already whole and complete, perfect and powerful, with flaws that actually make me special; a real woman.
- I listened to my inner voice telling me to take my rightful place in the world.

Women must claim their power now, not just because it is the right thing to do. Claiming their power is the only way women can heal the world and restore balance to this planet, which needs to reclaim the sacred feminine to survive. If we feel it, we can heal it! I have found happiness because I now know that self-confidence and self-love have nothing to do with what happens outside myself. Self-love is believing I matter because I say so. No one else can define me.

I claim my God-given right as a creator and I create my destiny by giving life to the life of my dreams—with my words. I am loved and matter because I say so. I have the life of my dreams and a life I love because I say so! I am lovable once and for all, because I say so!

MARGO DE LEÓN is a motivational speaker and author. She is a member of the National Speakers' Association and Toastmasters International, where she served two terms as an area governor. Recently, she was recognized with the "Distinguished Toastmaster Award," the highest honor Toastmasters International bestows on its members. Margo is working to complete her degree in family counseling and is currently a club officer of Voces Latinas Toastmasters club, which holds the coveted President's Distinguished title. She lives in Monterey Park with her husband, three sons and daughter.

www.margodeleon.com

The Pillar that Would Not Crumble

THEY SAY PEOPLE CAN REVEAL MUCH ABOUT THEMSELVES by telling the first memory of their lives. I am willing to share my first memory because each time I tell it, I grow stronger in spirit. Today, telling my story allows me to celebrate moments of joy; whereas once it did nothing but unleash wounded demons.

The incident happened when I was three years old, and it scared me. My fear haunted me for a long time, but I know now that my little memory was like a seed containing lessons I needed to learn about life. Within the seed was another seed that contained the wisdom and all the tools I would need to understand what happened to me. The release of the second seed would come only with time. It would be up to me to water it, feed it and nurture it to grow strong enough to lift me up from my tendency to self-destruct.

It happened late one night as I slept in my tiny bedroom, wearing my favorite pink and white pajamas that grandma had made for me. At the time I lived with my grandparents. I remember the loud, intrusive noise of the phone ringing and disturbing our little household. Grandpa answered. His voice sounded strained and confused. I slid out of my bed and shuffled into the living room. I wanted to see what was upsetting him. Who was he talking to?

"Stay where you are," he said to the secret person on the other end of the phone. "We'll be right there." Grandma stood next to him, holding her hands together as if in prayer. "We have to go get him," he said to her. "We have to go now."

Grandma put my coat over my pajamas and carried me to the car. It was dark. We never went out in the dark but this night we were in our coats, in the car, rushing down the street. Little did I know that we were on our way to fetch my darkest nightmare. It was the night we brought Uncle BiBi home.

I don't remember where we went or how we got my uncle in the car. I must have fallen asleep. My next memory was being home. Grandma was taking off my coat. She motioned toward him with a nod. "That's your uncle, *m'ija*," she said. "This is BiBi."

I saw him lying in the middle of the living room floor, face down, his arms to his sides with palms upward, as if he faced surrender and shame at the same time. He talked with a strange mumble and an occasional shout. He was upsetting my grandparents and me. I remember thinking, *Go home, whoever you are. Leave us alone.*

My Impossible Task

BiBi did not leave that night; in fact, he stayed well into my teens. BiBi wasn't drunk only for that first night; his drunken stupor continued for most of my young life.

Living with BiBi was like being a seedling striving to grow in the middle of the battleground between good and evil. I was a target for the disturbance that lived heavily inside his heart. Like a sponge, I absorbed a version of the darkness that invaded his spirit. I learned to see the world through the eyes of unhappiness and shame. I loved my grandparents. Him, I loved and hated at the same time. I came out of that home at war with the emotions of love and hate. Somehow, I usually ended up on the side of hate. I didn't think I was worthy or deserving of love. It was a complicated balancing act for a little girl.

I really wanted to like BiBi. I wanted him to like me, but the push-pull of it took a toll on us. He was usually mean when he was drunk, yet sometimes he could be fun. He would make us laugh. We would play games or go on an adventure with my cousins. It was as if he wanted to be happy. The desire was there, yet unhappiness always found him, no matter how hard he tried to hide from it. Often, I saw his laughter turn into tears and then back to laughter again. Because of BiBi, the line between happy and unhappy was often blurry for me. I wanted him to be happy. I thought it was my job to make him happy; but I failed. At eight years old, I already thought I was a failure.

I was convinced that BiBi thought I was ugly. He never said it out loud, but I could tell by the way he frowned when I was around him that no matter what I did or how I looked, I could never earn his approval. Even on Easter Sundays when I was nicely dressed with my bonnet, white dress and shoes, he looked at me with disgust. While everyone else thought I looked like an angel, BiBi ignored me.

Not even my ideas could get his attention. I tried very hard to come up with fun things to do. I thought of games to play or art projects to create, and he would laugh at me. His opinion of me was clear: I was ugly and worthless.

He was not the only one. The world outside my grandparent's home was no kinder. I didn't have any friends in school. School was just an extension of what was going on at home. One day it got too big. I gave up and threw in my tear-stained towel. I wanted to surrender and stop fighting the pain of my reality. I had been exposed far too long to my uncle's perception of the world and me. I knew I lost the battle when I began to agree: yes, I was ugly. I was awkward. My green eyes were far too big. They bulged. My short, thick hair looked like a brown helmet. The world gave me all the proof I needed to support this new-found truth. In school, I was the target of many jokes and pranks. At home I felt wounded when I should have felt sheltered. I hated that BiBi was right about me. I didn't deserve a good life. I felt worthless. I just wanted to find a hole and disappear.

I was thirteen when I fell into my own private abyss. I did a lot of thinking in my darkness. I wanted to know why I was born. What was my worth, my purpose? Did I have meaning? I didn't know my story. Who was I? These questions marched in and out of my head. They were strong and relentless—and everything depended on the answers, even though they might be contradictory, painful and devastating.

There was only one way out of the abyss. I had to find a way to believe I was worth something.

"You were born because you are a miracle," grandma answered.

"I don't know why you were born," BiBi mumbled between drinks. "Who cares?"

When I asked my mother, she became distant and grew quiet. What does a thirteen-year-old do with the silence? What did it mean? How could I not let that silence affect my perception of myself?

"Mom, why was I born?" I asked again.

Silence. And so I fell deeper into the abyss.

Even while in the jaws of darkness I continued to look for answers, especially from my mother. I was convinced she held the truth about me. I stood before her bedroom door knowing she was in there, silent. I knocked while suppressing the howling inside me. I calmly asked, "Mommy, can I come in?" I got no answer, just more silence.

I didn't always know what to do with my mother. She was different from other mothers. We lived under the same roof; therefore, she was there. Yet she wasn't there. She was busy working, going to school and pursuing a social life. Sometimes she would visit with me, but it was usually at grandma's insistence. Most of the time her life was closed to me. No time, no time at all for little Margo and her nonsense. This was the mother I knew. Was this normal?

Many years later I learned that my mother was very young when I was born. My parents were a teenage couple. Their elders had decided they were not ready to bring a baby into the world, so the story goes. My father's family was Cuban and Japanese; my mother's was Mexican American. Both sides were devout Catholics. Abortion was out of the question.

In the 1970s a young, unwed, pregnant girl was a family problem. These girls would often disappear on a nine-month "vacation." They were off to visit an "Aunt Mary" in Illinois. That was the story told to anybody who asked. However, my mother didn't have an Aunt Mary in Illinois, so she checked herself into St. Ann's Hospital, a hospital for unwed teenage mothers.

I was born there, but I was born a mistake. Arrangements for the rest of my life were made there. My mother put me up for adoption. I think it is ironic that it took another mistake to shape the life God had in mind for me.

The morning after my birth, the attending nurse forgot to read my mother's chart. She didn't see the instructions —ADOPTION—or that I was not to be brought into the room with my birth mother.

"It's feeding time," she told my mom. My mom didn't say anything, but instead took me in her arms. The nurse handed her a bottle filled with warm formula. She fed me. Once that happened, there was no way she was going to let me go. She knew it would be hard to face her parents with her decision to keep me.

Initially, my grandparents didn't want my mother to keep me. They wanted what was best for their daughter—and that didn't include being a young, unwed mother. They resisted her desire to bring me home, yet my mother stood her ground. Family came together and found a way to help us. My mother went home with my grandparents while I lived with foster parents for a while. I was able to come home with my mother and grandparents on the weekends. Monday through Friday I lived at the foster home and did so until my mother finished Catholic high school. I was a secret that needed to be kept from the nuns; if they found out, my mother would have been expelled from school. Eventually I came home for good. I was two.

Temporary Joy

I loved living with them. I was special to my grandfather. He was my superhero.

To me, he could do anything. Around him, I felt important. We would sing and dance. He taught me to swing dance and do the jitterbug. I loved it when he would swing me in the air and slide me on the floor. Sometimes we would fall together and laugh. I grew up loving the songs of the forties and fifties. However, when it came time for him to drive his truck across the country, life became dark, and I was lost again. No matter how much I begged and cried, grandpa had to leave and I'd slip back into my abyss until one day I couldn't come out. Not even for grandpa.

My abyss was a pit of terror. I was afraid. Without grandpa to protect me, I felt like living prey for a vulture named BiBi. Grandma loved me, no doubt, but she was afraid, too. We were both afraid of him.

One day BiBi came home very drunk. Grandma and I sat in the living room. We could hear him approaching the back door, talking loud and violently knocking over grandpa's garden tools. He crashed through the screen door yelling until his face turned red. Grandma took my hand and hurried us into the hall closet, where we hid until the house went silent and all I could feel were my bones rattling.

I was fourteen and the world was unclear to me. It was like living in a fog of uncertainty with occasional passing clouds of clarity. I felt my life sink lower and lower into darkness until even the occasional clarity diminished. Next thing I knew, I was emotionally sitting next to BiBi with the same crummy outlook on life. I didn't drink, but I had a mind-altering addiction. My drug was self-hate. It was taking me down until one day everything changed. I saw a way out of the abyss. It was a flash of light that came in the shape my cousin, standing in the middle of our living room. Donna came for me that day.

Donna was my cousin. She was four years older than me, and I looked up to her. She seemed to have everything in control. She had a radiant smile that made her beautiful and popular. I don't know what made her come to see me every day at noon that summer, but each time she arrived, I was pulled out of the abyss. I knew that she loved me.

We drove around in her car with the sunroof open. She talked about boys, clothes, makeup and music. She opened up an entire world that I had not known existed.

"You're a beautiful girl, Margo," she said to me one day as we drove down Sunset Boulevard. I don't remember why she said that. Maybe I was asking all those questions again that pivoted on my self-worth. "Don't you ever forget that." She glanced at her rearview mirror and smiled at the car full of good-looking boys behind us.

"Sometimes I feel ugly," I confessed to her.

"You're not ugly," she said. "Find a way to believe that. No matter what happens, be strong inside. Always be a pillar of strength. Don't let people take you down."

"I don't know how to be strong like a pillar," I said.

As soon as I said that, she pulled into the Tommy Burgers parking lot. She grabbed her purse and took out a tube of lipstick. It was a pretty shade of pink. "Put this on." She lowered the sun visor and pulled the mirror down behind it. I saw myself in the mirror; it was the familiar face I had grown to despise. I followed her orders and slid the lipstick across my bottom lip and then the left top and right top, just like I had often seen her do. "Press your lips together." She demonstrated, then pulled out a lip liner and applied the finishing touches to my lips. She fluffed up my hair and pinched my cheeks. "Now look in the mirror again," she ordered.

That can't be me, I thought. I looked pretty. I saw a side of me I had never seen before. There was actual light in my eyes. There was life in my smile. Tears formed slowly. I wanted to cry. I was human after all.

"That is how you become a pillar of strength," she said. "You pull yourself up. You do something about it. If you don't do it, nobody will."

Suddenly the car full of boys that had been following us parked next to our car. They piled out and dashed to our windows to talk to us. They thought we were pretty. We flirted. We smiled. We gave them hope and then we drove away.

"I told you," she laughed as she whipped around the corner onto Sunset Boulevard. "I told you, you were pretty. Did you see how the guy at your window kept looking at you?"

A flash of hope sped through my body like lightning. Could it be true? Was it possible? Could I one day be a marvelous woman like Donna? I wanted to believe this so bad it hurt.

Something new and exciting had just happened to me. It was as though Donna had breathed life into my lungs and I had come alive. Yet, when I looked at her while she laughed and her long hair flowed in the wind out her car window, I realized this was just another fun day for her. I wanted my life to be fun every day, too.

We drove home laughing with Van Halen blaring through our stereo. We turned heads. We teased. I felt powerful. I had climbed out of my abyss. That day, I loved my life like never before.

Donna came to hang out with me almost every day that summer. She helped change me. She taught me more about living like a pillar of strength. Every day she found a new way to say, "You pull yourself up. You do something about it."

A new me came to life. I started to like myself. I knew I wasn't the prettiest girl in the world, but thanks to Donna, I also knew I wasn't ugly. I thought Donna's influence over me would never end. She would always be around and we would have the rest of our lives to experience so many things. Our kids would grow up together and we would vacation together.

All these beautiful dreams came to a halt. Donna graduated from high school and went off to start her life. She left me behind with BiBi. The possibility of stumbling back into the abyss was real. The clouds rolled back in the shifting darkness. I lost myself again.

The Mouth of the Abyss

I was eighteen and still living at home. Living with BiBi required the ability to tread carefully. As long as you didn't push the wrong buttons, you could walk around him without incident. The problem was that a button could always be found where he was concerned.

For example, one day I was doing laundry. To get to the laundry room, I had to walk past his room. I must have stepped on a button somewhere along the way, because suddenly he started to yell at me.

"Are you stupid?" he shouted. "Why are you running the dryer? It's a hundred degrees outside. Hang your ugly stuff outside on the clothesline, dumbass!"

Strange, but my body started to tremble. It was fear, old childhood fear. My mind started to sink, and the mouth of the abyss suddenly opened wide to welcome me home where I belonged.

Suddenly Donna's words came back to me. *Be a pillar of strength.* The hairs on the back of my head stood up and I saw red. I put my basket on the floor and made my way to his room. I stood two inches from his face. "I am eighteen now," I announced. "I am an adult. If you have something to say to me, you talk with respect."

He didn't say anything. He stood silent, probably from shock. I began to walk out of his room. Halfway down the hallway, I heard him rushing toward me. I turned and pushed him down. To my surprise, he went down easily. He had no body mass. He was like a feather. He fell so hard he hit his head on the ground. Suddenly, bottled-up anger cut loose from inside of me. I told him he was nothing but a bully. I went after his record collection—Buddy Holly, Chubby Checker, The Temptations, all the others—threw them to the floor and stomped on them. I stomped until there were no records left to break. He just laid there staring at me. My grandparents stood silent. As I walked away, I heard them tell BiBi it was time to leave me alone.

After that day, as long as I lived in that house, I never spoke to my uncle again. A year later, I moved out.

If my first memory is a reflection of the greatest challenge in life, then overcoming my self-hatred could only happen as I learned to believe in myself over time. Inside the first seed was the challenge to acknowledge myself: an independent being separate from BiBi or anyone else. I needed to see the line where BiBi ended and I began. His anger hurt, but it was *his* anger, not mine. Now I knew my own anger.

Confronting BiBi was necessary. I put an end to his use of my soul as battleground for his pitiful war. I decided my life was mine and that it had purpose. I could no longer tow the burden of BiBi's salvation. I had carried this absurd cargo since I was a little girl. It was time to tend to me.

My task at hand was to rebuild my life. This time I would not use BiBi's perception of life whatsoever. I began to build my pillar of strength brick by brick. I structured the heart of my pillar from the love that had always been there: my grandparents'. My mother's decision to bring me home with her instead of giving me away was another brick I placed close to the heart of my pillar.

My pillar began to take shape. It was the beginning of the second seed. I longed to create a more worthy definition of me and my life. Certainly, rebuilding from the ground up was a challenge, and it was scary, but I worked very hard on it. I still had insecurities, and the little girl inside me occasionally still wept quietly at night. Yet I was getting stronger about who I was and what I was worth. For a long time I thought building my pillar —my strength—was my main task, but there was more. I began to realize that anger can fuel your need to survive, but a real life does not happen until you acknowledge the power of love.

Ditching Insecurities

Is there such a thing as happily ever after? My first marriage started out like a fairy tale. I was nineteen and in love. We had romance and all the trimmings. I gave birth to my amazing and gifted son, Román. I had learned by now how to be self-sufficient and stand up for myself. I was a pillar of strength, just like Donna had taught me to be. I was not going to be pushed around by anybody. But maybe that backfired, since a marriage is supposed to be about compromise. Donna didn't teach me how to do that.

Maybe I was a little too tough. The marriage didn't work out. Somehow my husband wasn't making me happy and he claimed I wasn't making him happy. We parted ways and went through an amicable divorce. After a while, I went through what most single people go through while looking for Mr. Right. I was dating, being encouraged, being discouraged. I had a hard time trusting men. Were they all here to reflect my lack of self-worth? If so, they were the enemy, and I was careful not to let them too close. I especially stayed away from men who drank.

My girlfriends took me out to celebrate one night after my divorce was final. It's amazing how fate works. I came so close to not going. I was just not in the mood for a "meat market" night, but I love to dance. It's a stress relief grandpa taught me to use. I needed a stress relief. I needed to dance. It turned out to be a wonderful night. I danced to great music, drank a few Coronas and I met Carlos. My equal.

At the bar, I stood ready to order another Corona, when Carlos walked into my space. He surprised me with what he does best. He pulled the best out of *me*.

"Do you mind if I hide out here?" he asked, looking to his left and his right, as though he were being followed. "They're looking for a single man, not a couple. If I stand here for just a second they will walk right past."

"What are you talking about?" I fought back a smile. He was cute.

"My insecurities," he said. "They follow me everywhere. How about yours? Did you ditch them yet?"

The rest of the night was so much fun. He wasn't drunk. That was important to me. This tall, handsome, nice guy was making me laugh. He made me think and kept me entertained with stories and jokes. Just as I began to think he was a lighthearted man, he would say something profound. He was and still is a delightful combination of both worlds: levity and depth.

Yet even with Carlos' wonderful resume, my demons haunted me. I couldn't trust him. I was afraid he would eventually turn and hurt me. I believed that men urged you to lose yourself in them. I was certain Carlos was no different from the other men I had dated. Toward the end of the night he asked for my number. I gave him a fictional name and phone number. I let him kiss me and then I walked away. I didn't want to believe in that kind of love. I reserved love for family.

Two weeks went by. I had tried to forget about the tall and dashing Carlos. My friends and I decided to go out for another night of stress relief. We had a great night. We danced, drank cold Coronas at the bar and enjoyed the music. Then I turned on my bar stool and there he stood. He startled me.

"What are you, a barfly?" I asked. "A permanent fixture?"

"I have a few questions to ask you, too, my dear," he replied. "Like, what is your real name? I saw your friends here last weekend. To my embarrassment, they corrected me on the subject of your name, *Margo*." He enunciated my name.

My friends. Oh gosh. This was their hangout. Of course they would have bumped into him. I could feel my face heating up. I knew it was probably red by now, but the lights were dim. Perhaps he wouldn't notice.

"I don't tell everything about myself the first time I meet a guy," I retorted. "Is there a 'meat market' law against that?"

"I just expected the truth out of someone I thought was special." He walked away, seemingly annoyed with me.

I swung my stool around, giving Carlos my back. I let my eyes fixate on a bottle of scotch on the top shelf behind the bar. I had read somewhere that the "top shelf" was expensive, the best stuff. Was I top shelf? I didn't feel top shelf at that moment. My defensive self felt justified in betraying him, but my heart was telling me something else. For some reason I liked this man. He was different, special, but my defenses made me lose any chance I might have had with him, and I had ruined my stress relieving evening, too. I decided I wanted to go home. Even the Corona didn't taste good any more.

I swung the barstool around and was looking for my friends when I saw him standing at the end of the bar talking with a group of men. I slipped off the stool having no plan, no retort, nothing in mind to say. The only thing I knew for sure was that my feet were walking toward him. As I approached, he looked at me with the most beautifully sincere eyes I had ever seen. We connected with that gaze.

"Do you mind if I stand with you for a bit?" I asked. "I'm not very good at ditching my insecurities. Maybe hiding here will help."

He grinned. His arm went around my shoulders. I melted into the strength of his arm and snuggled into the warmth of his chest. He felt right. We were a perfect fit. Suddenly I knew I was safe. Safe from falling into the wrong kind of love.

Carlos and I began to build our own beautiful life together. My son Román and Carlos got along really well. As far as Román was concerned, Carlos was his dad. I soon discovered I was pregnant with our daughter, Loren. Together we had a charming little house, our two children and our entire future ahead of us. Life was getting sweeter and sweeter for me every day. I was learning to love myself through my little family. I was learning that love is a miracle and I deserved to be loved.

I hadn't heard from Donna for quite some time. I knew she was married and stayed close to her home and husband. I didn't take it personally. I knew that when she was ready she would look for me. I was always ready to take her back into my life.

I guess I waited too long. One day when I was visiting my grandma, she told me Donna was sick. Her doctors and specialists told the family she had a severe case of pulmonary hypertension. I knew this was a serious disease inflicted upon my Donna. What would happen to her? The news shook me up.

I had my daughter, Loren, in my arms when grandma told me this. It seemed life went from cinematic color to grey and slow motion. I put Loren into her highchair and began to pace the kitchen floor. It's amazing how fast the human mind can think. Thoughts were flying through my head at record speeds. *Not fair*, my mind kept repeating. Emotions and memories dashed in and out. I wanted to cry, scream and jump into my car all at the same time. It was Donna and she was in trouble. It wasn't fair. She was only thirty. She had so much inside her yet to give. I knew firsthand she was a fountain of love and healing for anyone who needed it. I didn't want her to be seriously sick.

I had to get to her. Now I had to be that fountain of love and healing for her as she had been for me. I rushed home and put Loren into my husband's arms. I ran to my car, telling him, "It's Donna; she needs me. She's very sick. She may not make it." As I said the words, I felt myself go numb and I stopped in my tracks. My legs were jelly. I couldn't move a muscle. There is a lot to be said for denial. Or was it faith? All I know is that the minute I told myself, *She is not going to die. She is going to be fine,* my legs could move again.

I expected a miracle. As I drove myself to the hospital, I prayed and truly expected God to save Donna. I wanted to believe there was no time to cry because my dream of our families being together and both of us growing old together was so strong. "Yes, God," I prayed. "There is plenty of time for us."

I didn't know what to expect as I entered the room, but I took a deep breath and found her propped up in her bed. She was attached to many wires. An oxygen mask covered her face and she was breathing fast. I glanced at the heart monitor to check her pulse. It was in the forty-four to forty-five range. I knew anything lower than a fifty was dangerous. I was so scared but I kept telling myself that she was young and that God wasn't done with her yet.

I smiled at her and she motioned me forward. I leaned in to hear what she wanted to say.

"Tell everybody to leave me alone for a while. They make me nervous, but I want you to stay."

I nodded but noticed how winded she got on just those short sentences. "Don't talk anymore," I told her. "Let me do the talking. You just nod or shake your head, okay?"

She nodded.

I relayed her message to the family, and they left me alone with her. We spent the rest of the day talking. Actually, I did all the talking and she listened. I combed her long beautiful black hair. After all, Donna liked looking her best. I dug into my purse and pulled out my favorite light pink lipstick and applied it to her lips and she giggled. I pinched her cheeks and fluffed up her hair. I laughed; she smiled.

"Be a pillar of strength, Donna," I whispered in her ear. "Pull yourself out of this."

Her eyes quickly looked up to meet mine, and she went sad. Had she forgotten what she had taught me? Could it be that what had been so meaningful in my life had been forgotten by her? I didn't want her to see me cry. I looked away. I busied myself with placing my make-up and hairbrush back into my purse. I promised her I would be back the next morning. I hid my face as I wiped my tears. When I turned back to her, I noticed the sadness in her face had gone. She smiled and nodded as I kissed her forehead and said goodbye.

Exhausted and emotionally drained, that night I fell into a deep sleep. At 3:00 a.m. I woke up. In the darkness and silence of the whole house, I felt a cool sensation slowly caress the left side of my face. It felt comforting, like love. Peace. I suddenly thought of Donna. I went into a panic. I could hardly breathe. I wanted to call the hospital, but Carlos talked me out of it.

"She's asleep. She's trying to rest. Don't bother her." He tried to calm me down.

I knew I needed to sleep so I could be with Donna at daybreak. I let myself drift into a slumber. The next morning while making breakfast the phone call came.

It was the "nightmare phone call." You know the one, the call that makes a room heavy with silence even while you're standing in the middle of a busy household. It was the phone call you cannot challenge because it doesn't acknowledge you. It doesn't care what you want. It forces you to take it. Just take it. No choice. Just stand there and hurt.

The call was from my mother. She said Donna was dead.

I refused to believe it. "No!" I said over and over again. There was no way she was gone. Not completely gone. Right? Suddenly my denial turned to anger. *Not fair! Not fair!* How could God take her?

My heart tore open as I collapsed into a kitchen chair. I began to go over and over our last moments together. What had that sad look on her face really meant? Had she known? Why couldn't she have been a pillar of strength? Why had she given in? I wanted to scream, but instead I just cried. Everything that had ever hurt me came out that day. It was like someone had pried open a coffin and every ounce of pain inside of me rushed out like ghosts fleeing a prison of injustice. I had lost my hero. I was left alone, on my own. Donna had always been a safety net in case I fell close to the old abyss. Now the net was gone.

A Rich Soul

The day of her funeral, I tried to be a pillar of strength. It was hard to do. I felt like an empty shell. I couldn't cry anymore. I just wanted to fold, to curl up into the fetal position, lie down in a corner and be alone. Instead I tried not to think or feel anything, at least not until my heart could find a way to close back up.

"She was so young," people were saying. "She had just gotten married," someone else said, "and celebrated her second anniversary this year. Now her husband is alone."

I walked away from the talk. It was too depressing. I found myself walking toward Donna. I had previously tried to avoid seeing her in her coffin, but I was being drawn to it. Reluctantly, I stood before her. She looked asleep. I wanted to turn and walk away. That is not how I wanted to remember her. I wanted to remember her laughing, with the wind in her hair, her radiant smile lighting up and exposing the abyss. No fear.

For some reason I was held there before her coffin. Then I heard her say, "When you love, you forgive. Sometimes you have to let go, Margo. Forgive."

My heart skipped as it recognized her. She had come back to talk to me, but why did she want me to forgive her? There was nothing to forgive. To forgive is to first condemn, and I had never condemned her. I didn't understand, but I held her words close to my heart. "When you love, you forgive."

Carlos led me away from her coffin and into our car. "The procession is starting," he said.

The procession was huge, at least two hundred cars. Carlos drove and I sat in the front with him. My grandparents sat in the back. Grandpa was looking behind us at the cars that followed. "You know how rich a soul lived by the size of their funeral procession," he said.

That was truth if I ever heard it. Donna was a rich soul. So many people cared for her. She touched many lives. I could only hope to accomplish half of what she had done. I wanted to follow in Donna's footsteps. I wanted to help guide people to understand themselves and the world they lived in, but first, I had to learn how. I needed to heal. I was a willing follower. I wasn't sure who I was following but I had a feeling I had not really lost my safety net. Somehow, I felt Donna was still around.

I finished medical assistant school. It took me long enough, because I attended school while also being a wife and mother. I was hired by Health Care Partners, the second largest medical group in California.

As the assistant to Dr. Emmett Smith, my job was not only to assist his examinations but to take and report patients' vital signs, such as pulse, respiration and blood pressure readings. I enjoyed being a medical assistant and I liked my coworkers.

My social skills improved, and my self-worth grew stronger. I was interacting with people with greater ease. I was becoming

THE PILLAR THAT WOULD NOT CRUMBLE

independent and competent. It was quite an accomplishment for someone like me, who for so long had trouble believing in herself. Donna would have been proud. But if there was ever a day that I truly needed her magic, it was the day BiBi came back into my life.

I looked over the charts that I had prepared the night before and compared them to the day's schedule. There were some add-ons—patients who had been added to the schedule since the last check—and then I saw the name, Charles V. De León.

"No way," I thought. "It must be a mistake."

I double-checked the computer. There it was, clear as daylight. Charles V. De León, a.k.a. BiBi.

I was mad, but mad at whom? God! Oh, I was mad at God. Why? Because I had finally found a safe place in the world that was entirely my own, a world I had created not associated with any part of my past—neither my darkness nor its source. Then *he* showed up. I could see the abyss itself coming to claim me in my safe haven.

I went into an empty exam room and closed the door. It was time for a one-on-one confrontation with God. I looked up to the ceiling as if He were in the stucco.

"Where are you?" I asked. "We need to talk."

Silence. "Are you crazy?" I went on. "Do you really want World War III in this clinic? Out of all the clinics in Southern California, and of all the offices and doctors in this building, you bring him here, to me? Why? Send me a sign. What do you want from me?"

Donna's smiling face flashed through my mind. "What does that mean?" I shook her image away. I needed a quick solution to my problem, not Donna's love. Not right now.

I had to think fast. I ran to Mary, the only friend at the clinic I had who could keep a secret. I quickly explained my situation and asked if she would help me by assisting this particular patient whenever he came. She said she would help, but they had to explain to the two doctors we were assisting. Thank goodness both doctors agreed to go along with the plan. We kept this up for almost four months, but eventually everyone grew tired of it. I understood. It was unreasonable of me to hold my co-workers up as a shield against BiBi. One of the doctors, Dr. Smith, was right. It was time to confront my fears.

"Next time your uncle comes in," he said, "I will tell him you work with me and we'll give him the option to choose if he wants to continue his treatments here or perhaps move to another office."

That day came faster than I wanted it to. I walked behind Dr. Smith into the exam room, hiding, like a little girl again. What was BiBi going to do? Call me names? Would he tell Dr. Smith and all my co-workers that I was really just a stupid girl who shouldn't be trusted? Would they believe him?

Wouldn't it be funny, I thought, if this man turned out to be someone else? Maybe all this time it wasn't BiBi, just someone with the same name. I almost chuckled when we walked in but my high hopes quickly disappeared as I saw him sitting on the examination table. It was BiBi all right. He looked fragile, his body frail. He held his head low, as if in shame or surrender. Had he gotten smaller or had I gotten bigger? As I approached the exam table, Dr. Smith explained to him that I would be his medical assistant. I would schedule all of his appointments and have access to all of his medical records.

"Is that okay with you?" Dr. Smith asked him.

Bibi looked up at him and then over to me. Our eyes stayed with each other for a second. Then he looked down and nodded.

I took his vitals while Dr. Smith studied his chart. I could tell Dr. Smith was trying not to leave me alone with him. During the examination, I picked up BiBi's chart and could see that he was very ill. His liver was deteriorating at an alarming rate. Dr. Smith recommended that he live in a hospice facility.

The prognosis shocked me. I felt like I'd run into a brick wall. My anxious feelings about BiBi were suddenly blocked. He was a monster no more. Instead, he was vulnerable. Even after all that he'd done to me, I didn't want him to die. What did that mean for me? Would a part of me die with him?

I quickly slid out of the room and ran into the empty exam room where I'd petitioned God before. Guilt, remorse, love. I felt them all. Questions raced through my mind. Why? How? When?

Pull yourself together, Margo, I said to myself. *He is first a patient. Be a pillar of strength. This is not about you.* I said this over and over again to create the line, knowing that a line between BiBi and me existed. Boundaries. My codependent books emphasized the importance of boundaries. I needed this reminder. I needed to feel with my heart where BiBi ended and I began.

The gray spots in my heart started to clear up. Clarity started to dawn on me. I saw that the abyss that had owned me for so long had never been meant for me. It was his cloud. It had belonged to him all along. It followed him, not me. I just stood too close to him; I was a casualty. As a little girl, I took on his hell. Now I was braver. I wanted to save him. Tears fell from my eyes and I knew what I had to do.

All my life I had wanted to help BiBi, to make him laugh, make him happy. None of that was possible, until today. He was sick, and I believe he was delivered to me—that he came to me specifically—for help. This time, it was in my power to help. I promised him I would do everything I could to take good care of him. He nodded with a smile I had never seen before.

When Darkness Subsides

I took good care of BiBi. I promised myself he would be treated with dignity and respect in his last days. With each appointment, BiBi and I grew closer. We rebuilt our relationship upon a new foundation. I was finally able to see past his darkness, his depression as a cry for help, instead of an attack on me. As I got better at dismissing my fears, I was able to penetrate the wall he had built so high around himself in a vain attempt to keep the demons out. For thirty minutes once a week, I was the only one in my family he let into his world.

"When you love, you forgive." Donna's words stayed with me. Was I on my way to forgiving Bibi for all the years of mental anguish he had caused me? Could I leave that part of my past behind me? Let it go? I wanted BiBi to forgive, too. I knew he needed to find his seed and forgive who caused his original pain. I did everything I could to help him out of his depression. When I was with him, I gave him my love in abundance. I thought he was healing from the inside. I thought he was coming out of his abyss just like me. We talked about family. His smile showed me he truly loved them. We talked about Carlos and his silly jokes. We laughed and reminisced. I was highly optimistic, but I quickly learned that what happened in the doctor's office, stayed in the doctor's office.

That year, Thanksgiving was held at my grandparents' home. The house was filled with children, aunts, uncles, cousins and friends. The house was filled with laughing, joking and stories of past holidays. BiBi, however, disappeared. He stayed in his room. I wondered why he deliberately avoided these precious times. Actually, as far back as I could remember, BiBi never participated in family holidays. He often went out of his way to avoid them.

It seemed that BiBi had exiled himself from the family. At dinner that night, he quietly came into the kitchen to fill his plate and just as quietly returned to his room. Somewhere along the line, he had decided he didn't belong. I wanted to feel his pain and his loneliness. I wanted to reach out and make him feel better. There I was again, struggling to dip under his dark cloud to be in his world. I was drifting back to my girlhood, unsure again of the lines that defined and separated us. I sat back in my seat, took a deep breath and decided to let go of my need to help him. I decided to forgive him and love him from a distance.

My three-year-old daughter jumped on my lap and I understood the need to let go. I held my daughter close. I knew what she wanted. She wanted me to love her. I had taught her that. I also needed love from her. Affection wasn't always easily expressed by my mother. Yet, for me, the exchange of love was as important as the air we breathe. I promised myself that my daughter would never wonder if I loved her. The memory of the attention-starved girl I once was is nothing more than a numb recollection. To my surprise, there was no pain, no sadness. Forgiveness allowed me to pour out the love I had for my daughter and the gratitude to my mother for giving birth to me. I was free from the pain and the sorrow. I could enjoy this moment as we held each other, I accepted the joy that life was giving me. I accepted the life I had at that moment. I glanced at Carlos standing with grandpa in the corner of the kitchen, telling jokes and laughing. *Gosh, I love my husband,* I thought to myself. Those deep thoughts continued. *I am so lucky, so blessed. I have what I asked for. I chose my life—and BiBi chose his.*

Sure, it upset me that he chose sadness, and I knew he was just waiting to die. It was sad, yes, but his decision also deserved respect. It's what he wanted. I knew that. I had to accept it.

Since Donna's death, I was getting better at accepting reality. She had taught me so much, and I missed her. Memories of holidays past shot through my mind as I remembered how she lit up our house with her smile and laughter. I held my daughter closer, wishing she had known her. I fought back the tears and grieved some more. Then BiBi walked out of his room. Our eyes met as he walked toward the kitchen for a second helping. He smiled at me. I smiled back. Did he know that I finally understood him? Did he know I finally respected what he wanted? Did he know I had finally learned to love him? I looked at BiBi as he filled his plate with white turkey meat. His smile was gone and the look of inevitable defeat had taken its place. I couldn't help but wonder just whose death I was grieving at that moment.

Six days later, BiBi died.

To my surprise, BiBi's death shook me up. There I was again, at a coffin, looking at a loved one and trying to understand the meaning of life and death. "When you love, you forgive." I heard the words again. "Sometimes you have to let go."

Forgive? Forgive who, Donna? To forgive, you must first condemn. I no longer condemned BiBi.

"Not BiBi." Donna's voice was clear and strong. "You!"

Me? It was true. Then I understood. I was hard with me. I had condemned myself. I was quick to put myself down. I was quick to side with anybody's negative perception of me. I was quick to call myself a failure. Even when I put my fists up to fight anyone who condemned me, I agreed with them. I found some truth in their accusations—whether they were imagined or real. I needed forgiveness from myself. Could I forgive the funny-looking little girl I saw in the mirror for most of my life? Could I learn to love her? The thought of loving her stirred a whimper. I knew it was from her. This was the forgiveness I needed.

The truth is, when I was a little girl, I didn't know I was taking on BiBi's demons. It wasn't fair to be mad at me anymore. I simply had to draw the line, give back what belonged to BiBi and preserve what belonged to me.

It was my job to stop creating circumstances that caused my pain. I wanted to hug my little self, the part of me that thought I was ugly. I wanted to forgive myself for my self-condemnation. I wanted to finally feel safe inside of me. "I will miss you, BiBi," I whispered to him as a tear dropped onto my cheek.

"Poor BiBi," I heard Aunt Rachel mutter as she stood next to me. "He looks good, huh, *m'ija*? They did a good job."

I nodded and wiped a second tear from my cheek.

"I don't know when his life turned so bad. Maybe I'll never know" She said. She took a tissue to her eyes and nose. "This must be especially hard for you. You lived with him for so long, and he was your foster father and all that."

"What?" I asked. *What did she say?*

"Your foster father. They didn't tell you? Your uncle BiBi and your Aunt Sandra were your foster parents. They took care of you when you were first born. They kept you until you were big enough to live with your grandparents. Your *abuelos* were much too old to take care of a tiny newborn, so BiBi took you into his home. He loved having you. He told me he was amazed at how tiny your fingers were. He said you were an angel that had come to change his life."

Would the surprises surrounding BiBi never end? He thought I was an angel, here to change his life? Sometimes the mysteries of life were too much to try to decipher. It was hard to imagine BiBi happy at one time—a man with a wife, a foster child and a life. I tried to imagine him holding me in his arms, looking at my fingers and smiling. I couldn't do it.

I did, however, begin to see BiBi in a different light. Somehow, he became a different man. He became a man with a broken heart who had condemned himself to a hell no one else could understand. I wished he hadn't done that to himself. He was worth more than that. I would make sure his life counted.

"I will never forget you, BiBi," I said to my foster father as I walked away from his coffin.

If it is true what they say about your first memory, then I have revealed my very soul. The seed within that memory had lessons for me to learn and embrace. It taught me much about myself and my life. It showed me my own strengths.

I decided to believe that BiBi had always been there for me. He pushed me to the edges of darkness so that I would truly recognize light when it dawned on me. He was with me during my darkest hours and during the brightest light. Then he let go and released me to my family, so that I could be the best wife, mother and woman. He helped me forgive myself and heal so that I could be a teacher for those who hurt as I'd once hurt. Now I am willing to help others, just as Donna and BiBi helped me.

I love BiBi. I can say that now. I know he can hear me when I say *much of what he did was wrong*. It is not okay to be drunk and hurt people. It is not okay to disrupt a family and cause them to fear you. Forgiveness does not mean it's okay to continue hurting people or disrespecting their lives.

BiBi was on a collision course, ready to self-destruct. When you are determined to destroy yourself, it is not fair to take others with you. This was the lesson that caused me to stop wallowing in my self-pity and instead rebuild my inner pillar with love.

I learned that self-forgiveness is to know what is yours and let go of what is not yours. If you feed what hurts you and keep it alive, it will destroy your life, your relationships and even your health. It will taint your heart and fill it with grief until it becomes a darkness that swallows you: an abyss. You can pass a broken heart to your children, and because they trust you, they will take it in and make it their own. Or you can teach them to let go and forgive.

Let go of the hurt and pain and forgive yourself for holding onto it too long. Let it go to bring back the light and the joy you deserve. Let this be how you are remembered. Let this be what makes your funeral procession rich with love and spirit.

LAURA DE ANDA is a speaker, writer, editor and legal services broker. She has worked as an editor at several newspapers, including the *Los Angeles Times* and *Washington Post*. In the nonprofit arena, she has served as a club president and district officer within Toastmasters International, and also was a teen helpline trainer in Connecticut and a helpline volunteer in Texas and Rhode Island. She holds bachelor's degrees in communications and philosophy from Trinity University.

My Father's Daughter

I DON'T BELIEVE IN PRINCE CHARMING, BUT I BELIEVE in my father, who is a true hero. I don't want to be a mother but I love and need my mother. I don't want to be a housewife, yet the memories of my grandmother's sweet laugh and the delicious aroma of her *mole* still bring comfort to my soul. Together, their love and life's journeys have shaped me into who I am: I inherited the best of my father's beautiful mind, my mother's resilience and my grandmother's ability to love and nurture.

As a child, two possible journeys lay before me. One side held loss and disease, the other, fortitude and love. I lived on the healthy side for most of my youth, but at the age of ten I began to experience a darker side. My story is about the choice I made, nearly succumbing to the darkness and yet recovering. I can now stand tall, lift my head, open my heart and say I love my life.

But first let me tell you who I was.

Growing up, I visited the local library after school where I'd lose myself in the bookshelves. For fun, I enrolled in advanced math and logic summer classes. With my big eyeglasses, gap-toothed grin and freckles sprinkling my cheeks, I embraced my inner nerd. I valued brains over beauty.

As their first-born child, my father and mother poured their hopes and best wishes onto me.

Dad had a beautiful mind. As a self-taught man, my dad's books were his joy, especially his encyclopedias. Dad ended up collecting about a dozen sets and read each one, starting with the A's. Our family bathroom always displayed his latest selection. As he poured over his books, his mind was like the Library of Congress, so vast and full of knowledge. His best asset was his mind.

I often wondered why he found so much joy in reading. It wasn't until I grew older and discovered the same joy in good books that I could appreciate the adventures, histories and ideas within the pages. On the bookshelves were the products of the talents, research and imagination of writers who had dedicated their hearts into their works. I also theorized that Dad was filling the mental-stimulation gap in his job. Each day, he tightened bolts on the assembly line at the local air force base—repetitive, mind-numbing work. He often worked overtime and would get home late at night. Other days, he would come home, spend time with us while mother prepared dinner and then retire to his joyful reading.

As a child I loved school because my dad loved learning. He would encourage me to read and learn. He believed the privilege of learning should not be confined to school hours but should be a continual flow throughout one's life. Although he stopped his formal education at high school graduation, he never stopped learning. He had his reasons for encouraging his children to be educated. Both he and Mom learned to think and speak in Spanish. She learned English in elementary school while Dad took English as a Second Language classes and worked to minimize his accent. My dad, who felt embarrassed about his shortcomings with English and his struggles with school, did not want his children to struggle with the language. He believed a quality life could be found in the ability to speak and write immaculate English, coupled with a college education. He had his children's best interests in mind when he spoke only English at home, taking care not to speak to us in Spanish. He kept that beautiful language between him and mom.

"You're going to college," he said with confidence. He always inspired me to do more than he had achieved. "Be a doctor or a lawyer," he'd suggest, "I might need you." What he really meant was: *Make me proud. Fulfill my own unrealized dreams. Be the first in the family to get a degree.*

I was happy to earn my degree, not just for him, but for me.

One of the highlights of our family outings were car rides around town. Always the teacher, Dad turned these into educational excursions.

"What's the name of that street?" Dad asked, teaching us how to read street signs. "Texas?" I guessed. Yep, we happened to be driving on Texas Street in San Antonio. He enjoyed driving, usually testing out another used car he had bought from a local lot. Always in the driver's seat with Mom by his side and kids in the back seats, Dad would treat us to delicious Mexican plates from a local drive-in restaurant. If it was nice out, we'd drive to a nearby lake. During the summers we drove to Corpus Christi and South Padre Island. Family times were happy times.

I knew, very young, how much my family was cemented in my being. My father, my mother and maternal grandmother were the pillars that sustained me. They were my strength, my love source, my life line. I believed they would always be there; therefore so would I. Then one day something shook them. My pillars of sustainability began to waiver. The bold, unfeeling truth revealed itself to all of us one day at the dinner table.

I was ten the first time I witnessed it. It happened in grandma's kitchen. The intoxicating aroma of her enchiladas filled the entire house. I remember purposely expanding my nostrils to take in the smell of the melting cheese and the chili sauce wrapped in corn tortillas in the oven. I watched as grandmother served my dish.

"More *chile*, Grandma," I said. "I like it spicy."

"*Qué bueno*," she said as she chuckled and obliged, knowing how much I loved her cooking. All was well in the world when I was in grandma's company. She embodied love, acceptance and goodness. Her home, like our own family home, was a safe haven.

But that safety would be punctured by unseen forces.

Dad was acting differently. He was like a stranger. His jokes were gone and his smile was absent. His facial expression was rigid. The energy in the house had grown heavy and tense. He whispered to Mom far more than usual. Something was up, but what?

When the phone rang, Dad's face tightened.

"Don't answer," he instructed Mom. "They'll call back." After approximately seven rings the phone went silent.

Then the phone rang again. This time he counted the rings. "Don't answer it," he cautioned her.

When the phone rang a third time, he said, "Pick it up on the fourth ring, but don't say anything."

All of us at the dinner table began to count the rings with dad. At first we thought it was a game, but as it continued and I saw the stress on his face, I realized it was real to him.

Each time the phone rang, and it seemed to be ringing more than usual that day, our entire family was involved. We counted together and we learned to answer it on the fourth ring. It had to be the fourth ring, and the closest one to the phone would make a dash to answer it. Slowly the table grew more and more silent as we ate. The tension was strong. Our beige kitchen wall-phone had taken center stage over my grandma's delicious enchiladas. I could hear the warning bells in my head ringing that night. Something was wrong.

The Secret at Home

Everything had taken on new meanings for him. Dad attached a special code to everyday acts and only he possessed the combination. As the months went by and his suspicions continued to grow, our family learned just how serious his condition was becoming.

These incidents began to build momentum. He was growing more suspicious of strangers. Street signs had been replaced by imaginary signs meant to warn him of possible harms. Family car outings, which used to be fun excursions, were now used to validate Dad's growing fears.

"They're staring at me," he'd say about other drivers. "See that?"

One by one, oncoming cars were transformed into ominous stalkers in Dad's eyes.

"No, Dad. They're not staring at you," we'd assure him. But nothing could convince him otherwise. The voices in his head were louder than the voices outside.

He told us how he was receiving messages from TV commercials and the radio. He talked about being able to "send" messages in the same way. My dear father was creating his own way of interpreting the world and making sense of it. The thing is, it didn't make sense to anyone else.

Our family was becoming hyper-vigilant. We started policing ourselves, being careful not to send a wrong message with our actions. But how could we know how our behavior would be interpreted, when only Dad held the special code?

Dad's beautiful mind was beginning to torment him. He was closing himself off from the rest of us, alienating himself from everyone he cared about. He retreated into a private world with his radio and television, spending a lot of time in the den he had built years ago above the garage. He tried to understand and communicate with his new reality. But each attempt only upset him more and provoked more paranoia.

It was our family secret. My siblings and I didn't invite friends over. We thought we could control and work out our father's problem at home by bringing reason and logic to his fears. That didn't work. If we happened to be in the same room with Dad, we'd get an earful as he tried to process what was going on in his head by talking through his thoughts. Dad just wanted an ear, even if my eyes were glazing over when he spoke for what seemed like hours at a time. We realized his needs were far beyond what we could provide when he started acting on the delusions. One afternoon, he climbed into his Ford Bronco truck, reversed it and rammed it into the fence that surrounded our home, destroying what was once a fortress to him.

My father was fighting demons he could no longer slay on his own. He was confronting fears he could not see. He fought a losing battle. It was out of his control, and out of ours. He needed help, so I started to look for it. I was sixteen.

Help came in the form of a nameless, faceless telephone counselor. I called the local United Way Helpline, and explained to the volunteer what was going on. She suggested we consider involuntary commitment. This meant dad would be forced to get medical help and taken to a local hospital.

This was a heart-wrenching decision, but mom and I wanted him to receive treatment and hopefully his old self would return, the man we knew and loved. Mom wanted the man she had fallen in love with back in her arms.

They had met in the safety patrol and became junior high sweethearts and got married when she turned twenty-one. He was a tall, handsome, outgoing man who made her laugh. She was a warm, friendly, graceful woman who attended church with her parents. Just a few years after their small wedding, Dad used his savings to construct our family home, built with family love. With cold beers as incentive, he invited all my uncles and both grandfathers to build his castle.

Mom was his queen. But, now, the king was incapacitated. His queen needed to rescue him from his demons.

I drove with mom to the downtown courthouse to fill out the paperwork. A few days later, we waited anxiously at home, glancing at the clock during the two-hour window to expect the medics. We all pretended to be having a normal family gathering in the living room. It was a cloudy day outside and inside our home were clouds of dread. Dad was talking to us, still desperately trying to process the random thoughts that were bombarding his mind.

When the medics knocked on the door, my heart skipped a beat.

Oh no, what if something goes horribly wrong? I thought with dread.

My younger brother and two sisters were too young to understand, but they knew dad needed help. So the kids knew what was happening, but not dad. Who were these strangers? Dad looked confused and became even more guarded. His already active sense of paranoia was growing stronger and looming over all of us. We could see he was struggling with what was real, what was fantasy. He looked to us for an explanation.

The medics showed Dad the paperwork while Mom reassured him, "Honey, they're here to help you." Her voice was gentle and comforting.

I remember saying, "It's okay, Dad." But I didn't feel okay.

For the first time, I saw my father's vulnerable side. I immediately put myself in his place: to be the king of his castle and then to no longer be calling the shots. He had been doing his best to raise us, to earn money, and he had been stopped short of his goals.

The medics escorted my father out of the warm home and into a cold ambulance. He was gone.

I looked at Mom. "We did the right thing," I assured her.

My mind said yes, but the scared little girl inside hesitated. My body shook with fear as worst-case scenarios played out in my head. What if he'd be angry at mom and me for what we'd done? What if he can't be helped? What if he refuses help? Could he distinguish help when he thought everything was meant to hurt him? Would he ever trust us again?

After those negative thoughts passed, I breathed with relief. After all, dad would now be in the care of professionals. The energy of the house was noticeably lighter, as if an ominous dark cloud had been lifted. I knew I had to trust our decision was for his best. The hospital would help him and give us back our dad. I had to believe this.

The hospital did tests, examined my father and made a diagnosis. In a roll of the cosmic dice, my father had developed a chemical imbalance in his brain. Schizophrenia.

Head of Household

At the age of forty, my dad was forced to take disability retirement. The household income plummeted. My mom, who hadn't worked since shortly after high school, now relied on disability checks and food stamps to feed our family. My mother was brave. I don't know where she found the courage, but I could see it surrounded her like a cape. She was my hero. As I watched her take one day at a time, she was growing stronger each day. Now as head of the household, she did what she had to do to feed and protect her family.

One afternoon, I will never forget, we stood in line at the checkout counter. I helped my mother unload the groceries onto the conveyor belt. When the cashier rang up the total, Mom began to count the food stamp coupons from the book. I grew embarrassed as she counted out ones, fives, tens and twenties, and tore off the perforated coupons—an awful ripping sound. I felt the impatience of the people behind us waiting in line. I felt their judgment. I looked to my mother for support and I saw her stand before the cashier, composed and unwavering. Her face said, *This is a hand-up, not a handout. For my family, I will do what it takes to keep us fed.*

I felt my stance straighten. I strived to feel the same. Mom has always held the family together even as things were falling down around her. She was steady and steadfast. When the family's resources dwindled, her resourcefulness grew stronger.

When we were finally allowed to visit dad in the hospital, the roles had reversed. Like chess, the more powerful queen was protecting the restricted king. Dad's movements were now limited. Under a doctor's care, his freedom had been curtailed. When dad walked up to greet us, he seemed more in control than we'd seen him in months. His eyes were filled with yearning and caution. After some small talk with Mom, he said, "I don't belong here. Get me out of this place. I want to go home."

"I know you do," she looked away. "But, hon, that's not up to me."

"They will listen to you," he said. "Tell them I am better. Tell them you want me home now."

She turned to him and with great care and respect she said, "I love you and I miss you. As soon as the doctors say it's okay, you can come home."

Because of the nature of his illness, being in the hospital must have been a special hell for him. He was surrounded by strangers, no longer in the safety of his own home, with his freedom restricted. There had to be an easier, gentler way.

Homecoming

Dad finally did return home and he did what he could to recover. He obediently took the medications that doctors prescribed, but the side effects took their toll on his body. One would make him jittery, like a twenty-four-hour caffeine high. Another drug would make him sedate. He said he felt like he was walking underwater. It pained me to see him go through this agony.

This wasn't his choice; this affliction chose him. Through the years, dad learned to distinguish between thoughts that were based on reality and those that weren't. He was determined to recover.

I was very excited to have him home. I hadn't seen joy in my mother's eyes like I did on the day he returned. Dad, however, was distant. He would smile from time to time but mostly he was guarded. He kept to himself or stayed close to Mom. I would see them at times, eating dinner at the table. Their eyes would lock onto each other, for long moments letting their eyes do the communicating. His eyes would say, "Will everything be all right?"

Her eyes answered, *You are safe with me.*

My father's ordeal changed us all. We were not the same family. We were still close. We still loved each other, but circumstances rearranged our family dynamics. With time, my father learned how to control the illusions that had once overpowered him. My mother learned how to become self-sufficient and resilient. She even went back to work at a local elementary school. I had learned that the man of the house may not always be the provider or head of household. I learned that just because a man is a man doesn't mean he is indestructible. It doesn't mean he can't fall. He is human, after all.

My mother kept busy with my younger siblings and my father. I helped her the best I could, and I felt the best thing I could do was take care of myself, rely on myself. So, I spent most of my time at the local library after school. In my childhood years, the library was an enchanted land. Now, the library had become a refuge, another home away from home, where the friendly librarians greeted me by my first name and with a smile. This place was my oasis. I was surrounded by shelves full of books containing pages of infinite research, creative endeavors, opinions and biographies of many lives before me. Each time I opened a new book, my world expanded.

One of my favorite children's book was *Masquerade* by Kit Williams. Within this beautifully illustrated tale were clues to a jeweled 18-carat gold hare buried somewhere in the world. I became obsessed with solving this puzzle. Day in and day out, I would study the pages, attempting to decipher the poetic writing that would finally lead me to a hidden treasure. I never found that treasure, but I discovered a more powerful truth: I realized that the true treasure lies within.

Just like my father, I loved learning. I believed reading was the doorway to greater intelligence and awareness. In addition to delving into books, I enrolled in extra educational programs every chance I got. When I was twelve I attended a pre-engineering program at a local university and studied vector analysis and logic. In high school, I challenged myself with classes in advanced placement chemistry, geometry, algebra, computer science and biology at a special afternoon program offered at the local community college. My personal victories were excelling in school, winning academic contests and spelling bees. After the diplomas were earned and the formal classes ceased, I continued to feed my need to learn and collected books for my personal library. I was diligent with my education. I was building a mind that could not fall.

I believed in self-reliance. I knew there would be no Prince Charming coming to rescue me and provide my Happily Ever After. I scoffed at the Cinderella fantasy where some man would save me. I knew it was up to me. My mind would be my fortress. At seventeen years old, after graduating first in my high school class, I started working my way through college. I had applied for and earned scholarships and grants that made my bachelor degrees possible. I wanted more. My need for education and experience was insatiable. I wanted to explore the world. At twenty-one years old, I embarked on my chartered course of independence and moved to the East Coast to begin my journey exploring life's possibilities. There, I began work at a newspaper, the first of several in my print journalism career.

One of my first destinations outside of the United States was Mexico City. This trip beckoned me. I was sculpting my identity, and magnificent Mexico helped me to connect with the land and my ancestors. The ancient Aztec pyramids of Teotihuacán helped me understand that I came from a strong people. The majestic beauty of the mountains, the topography and the clear sky that brightly displayed the stars and their constellations in the dark of night were begging to live inside of me. I gladly let them in. My forefathers and mothers lived in this magnificent land deeply rooted in Aztec and Spanish culture and tradition. Pride in my genealogical roots went beyond the Spanish language, which I practiced daily. Growing up in the United States had reinforced my English, but my forefathers' language was like a sweet melody. Yes, I regretted not mastering Spanish when I was younger. Nonetheless, I savored every moment of my visit, which served to strengthen my life—body, mind and spirit—as a happy, independent woman.

Other travels took me to exquisite Europe. I marveled at the Sistine Chapel. I stood in awe and relished the skyscraping Eiffel Tower in Paris. I gasped when I first saw the sunlit views of the multicolored stained-glass windows at Sainte Chapelle. I marveled at the splendid intricacies at St. Mark's Cathedral in Venice and the stunning architecture found in Barcelona and Madrid. I basked in the glory of what the hearts and minds of mere human hands could create. I realized that human beings are capable of creating magnificent art and architecture. And I reveled in the magnificent splendor that Mother Nature created, in such places as Yosemite and Zion National Parks. With a newfound appreciation for the wonders of man and nature, I realized that beauty is everywhere.

Nontraditional Women

Long marriages run in my family. My parents have been married over forty years and both sets of grandparents were married over sixty years. My maternal grandparents' strong union survived the difficult years that my grandfather spent overseas, fighting in World War II, storming Normandy on D-Day. They shared in the laughter of their four sons and one daughter and their grandchildren. They attended graduations, birthdays, weddings—and also shared tears over the deaths of two sons.

As I left my teenage years and hit my twenties and thirties, the inevitable question arose: why did I remain unmarried?

My response was the same: "I just haven't found my equal." By "equal" I meant a wonderful partner who I admired and enhanced my life as I enhanced his. I had my list of must-have qualities and deal breakers. I valued kindness, compassion, honor and integrity. Most of all, he had to "get me," respect me and let me be me.

The men I'd dated possessed some of these qualities, but no one man had possessed all of the ingredients, so single I remain. I secretly feared the love of my life might change, through no fault of his own, like my father had. Instead of revealing my innermost fears, it was easier to laugh them off and assert my independence.

"I'm doing just fine on my own," I proudly declared to my friends and family. "I'm self-sufficient, happy and free, thank you very much."

Yet, as much as I enjoyed being on my own, I looked with pride at my grandparents' long and strong marriages. Call me a closet romantic, but I was fond of the fact that my grandfather affectionately called his wife *Reina*. That mutual admiration is the test of a true, strong marriage to me: when he views his life partner as his queen and she sees him as her king. Mutual respect and lots of love and laughter were the ingredients that strengthened their loving bond.

Did I crave marriage and children? Nope.

At first, the decision not to have children was a silent one. Our family had survived my father's ordeal, and I was left with no patience for fantasy or make believe. I was a stickler for truth and reality. Raising children, to me, required a great deal of fantasy that I didn't think I could provide. I had broken from the fairy tales told to girls about a prince coming to rescue us women. I knew this would never happen. I had never seen it happen in real life. My mother was no Cinderella or Snow White, but she was good at slaying dragons. My mother was more of a hero to me than Prince Charming could ever be. She was a Wonder Woman. I found myself wanting to be more like her in several ways, except for one: I didn't want to have children.

One day while visiting Grandma's house, the conversation turned toward one of my cousins, who was expecting a baby.

"I'm happy for her," I said as I reflected on my own child-free journey. "Gosh, Mom, you won't be getting any kids from me."

"Oh, that's all right, I don't want to be a grandmother anytime soon," Mom joked.

Grandma chuckled as she rolled out the *masa* for her handmade tortillas. "What's the hurry? You don't need to make this decision now," she said in broken English.

"Grandma," I braced myself for what I was about to say. "I just don't want to get married."

To my surprise, she smiled with approval.

"Whatever makes you happy," Mom said.

"I am happy," I replied as I took a bite of one of grandma's tortillas fresh from the hot stove burner.

"*Qué bueno*," Grandma chuckled.

I was glad they accepted me for who I was. I was thankful for their approval, and I also knew I didn't need it to proceed with my bold plans. Who was I to buck tradition? My mother was happy with children. Grandma was happy in her kitchen. Why didn't I trust what has made many women happy in centuries past and probably for centuries to come? To me, the traditional roles for women seemed confining. What if you built your life on motherhood or wifehood and then realized you hadn't created the life you truly desired?

My mother's and grandmothers' lives were filled with children, husbands and homes. My life would be filled with academics, professional careers and an entrepreneurial spirit. I humbly respected and honored their life choices, and I found joy playing the role of *tía*, "Auntie Lala," to my young nieces and nephews. I wanted more for myself. This decision felt right for me.

I've always been a firm believer in women's independence and also women's interdependence with men. I'm proud to see our culture embrace this mentality. I noticed this phenomenon as I watch my young niece's favorite animated films. The characters she was watching still included some of the mainstays, such as Sleeping Beauty and Cinderella, but the newer characters were strong females such as Mulan, Fiona, Merida and Pocahontas. This cultural evolution followed the footsteps of the Bionic Woman and Wonder Woman of my youth. Now these were women to admire and emulate. Imagine my delight when I discovered that the actress who portrayed this super-heroine, Lynda Carter, was Mexican and Spanish on her mother's side. That's right, a Latina Wonder Woman. It was enough to make a Latina grow wings and fly without limits. Come to think of it, most of the Latinas I know are wonder women. I was proud to be a woman, Latina, and free.

Then, my wings were clipped.

In early 2001, my grandmother complained of discomfort, but the first doctor who saw her suggested she take aspirin. When the pain increased, a second doctor's visit finally resulted in X-rays. It was cancer.

I felt the struggle inside my mind trying to understand how a savage beast could infiltrate the sweetness and gentleness of my grandma's body. She was an angel being ravaged by a monster. Grandma meant the world to me. She was also mom's closest confidant. There is a special bond between mother and daughter, and my mom was grandma's only daughter. In my eyes, grandma represented all that was good, kind and pure.

Throughout her life, my dear grandmother had put her faith in God. Even her laughter was soft and melodious. Like my mother, she always expressed kindness. In her small two-bedroom home, prayer-lit candles sat on a chest of drawers, burning with their soft glow. The top of this chest was a mini-shrine: hanging on the wall above this religious shrine was a picture of a guardian angel in a pink and green flowing dress, hovering over two children. Grandma had several rosaries, and on the walls were pictures of Jesus Christ and the *Virgen de Guadalupe*. To top it off, their home was only a stone's throw away from the Basilica of the National Shrine of the Little Flower.

But all of Grandma's faith couldn't stop a dreaded, insatiable disease from eating away at the insides of her stomach. The pain was excruciating, yet my grandma never whined nor felt sorry for herself. Blaming or complaining wasn't her style. The way she dealt with the pain was praying her rosary under her breath, putting her faith in God. She told my mom and the doctors that she felt "uncomfortable" and shifted her weight when she became bedridden. Throughout the numerous doctor and hospital visits, Grandma maintained her grace and dignity.

At the time, I was living and working on the East Coast. How I wished I could instantly be transported home to comfort my dear grandma and ease her pain. I wanted things to be the way they used to be, when my grandparents' house had always been my haven, a warm home filled with comfort and safety. Now that peaceful serenity was being ravaged by malignant cancer cells attacking her small, fragile body. And then she died.

When I got the phone call from my mom about grandma passing away, a part of me also died that day. I would never see her smiling eyes or hear her sweet laugh again. She was gone at eighty-two.

I should have been comforted by the fact that she was no longer in pain, and one part of me was. But a large part of me just wanted her back. A deep void was left where she had been.

The finality of it all struck me, and I wondered at times why an omnipotent God would allow bad things to happen to good people. If it was her turn to pass away, why would He choose such a painful way for her to die? How could such cruelty be allowed to happen to a peaceful, devoted woman?

All the mind-building strengths I had spent years and effort on were starting to disappear. My fortress, my beautiful mind and all my defenses started to crumble. I realized grandmother was still, and always had been, one of the pillars in my foundation. My father was keeper of one of the three pillars, and it wavered greatly during my adolescence. My mother's position as a pillar also wavered but stood strong nevertheless. Grandmother's death was final. She was gone. How could I be sustained? What happened to my power? I let her death from cancer shatter my spirit, and I went from happily invincible to frightfully lost.

Asking myself these disempowering questions only fueled the flames of my grief. As the days and weeks went by, I noticed I was becoming more and more incapacitated. The simple, everyday acts of getting out of bed, showering and going to work became challenging, tedious. What was once effortless now required all of my concentration to accomplish.

Just a few months later, on September 11, I found myself again being struck by life's delicate fragility. As I witnessed the endless CNN playbacks of planes crashing into New York's Twin Towers, I allowed those images of death and destruction to overpower me. The once towering structures were reduced to rubble, and along with the shattered skyscrapers, my own sense of self became unglued. The debilitating grief that I had unsuccessfully tried to suppress at grandma's funeral was triggered again and again with each news broadcast. In the post-9/11 world, life was tenuous.

The constant reminder of death and destruction flooded my entire being, leaving me feeling wounded, vulnerable and isolated. It was as if my body's release valve was switched on, and crying let out all of my despair and agony. The unfairness of life hit me: seeing my father's beautiful mind falter and watching my mother struggle to care for my father year after year. I wondered if I would follow in my dad's footsteps.

It all frightened and shook me. Most days after work, in the comfort of my apartment, I cried until there were no more tears, no more energy. I was being torn down while facing the fact that my life was full of fear, vulnerability, unpredictability and unbroken promises.

I wanted the past. I wanted things to be as they once were.

Everyday tasks continued to take tremendous effort. It took everything in me to get out of bed in the morning, shower, drive to work and focus. I felt strength rapidly leave my body and spirit. I was shrinking inside. It was as if I was living in a thick fog, as my movements seemed slower and more sluggish. I no longer found joy in simple pleasures because all of my focus and energy were on maintenance. I remembered that my father lost control bit by bit. Similarly, I felt like I had no control over my grandmother's death, the terrorist attacks, life in general.

I felt like I was losing control of my thoughts, too. Like father, like daughter?

My family and those closest to me noticed the change in my demeanor. Soon I was seen by doctors. They put a stamp on my forehead and prescribed pills. "Depression," they concluded. "Take this yellow pill every day. And this purple pill will offset the side effects of the first pill. All will be well." Depression? Not schizophrenia, but what was the difference? My beautiful mind was failing.

My often bumpy road to recovery lasted nearly a year. As someone who had never tried illegal drugs—or ever smoke or drank alcohol—I grew frustrated with the drugs' side effects. Their aim was to re-establish acceptable serotonin levels in my brain. All I noticed was that one medicine gave me excess energy, in the form of jitters. Another drug added twenty pounds to my petite frame. With each chemical came another unwanted side effect. I was getting another taste of what my dad had gone through years ago. I was my father's daughter.

On the therapeutic side, I talked with counselors, and one who specialized in cognitive behavioral therapy helped me most of all. When I often judged circumstances or incidents that happened to me as bad, or wishing for something different, he helped me to focus on my own thoughts. Were they helpful? If not, then let them go, he suggested. So I didn't have to believe every bad replay? This shift helped me to process what happened to me, but I was stuck in the past.

My friends gave me books to ease the pain, like Anna Quindlen's *A Short Guide to a Happy Life*. The books comforted me on an intellectual level, but I was still sick, still stuck. My soul was broken, my spirit was defeated. In moments of frustration, I'd tell myself, "Just snap out of it!" My sickness was at a cellular and spiritual level. I felt lost and emotionally bankrupt. My mind was saying one thing, but my body was doing another. I was a lethargic mess. I was at the breaking point, until the day my mother flew in to see me.

I lay in bed covered up with a comforter. My room was dark when Mom came in. I kept it dark because it felt better. I didn't want to see any more surprises. No more heartbreak. I heard her gently close the door behind her and switch on the lamp. I smelled her fragrant perfume as she came closer. I felt her sit on the bed next to me, but I laid still. She sat quiet for a while. I thought she might be praying. Then I felt her gentle hand rest on my shoulder.

"I miss her so much," I said through the tears.

"Oh, Laura," she said softly. "People die. Everybody dies."

Death seemed so final. All life ends in death? The thought of *her* dying caused a small flood of tears to burst silently from my eyes. I wanted to hug her and hold her close, so close where death could never pry her from my hold. But I stayed under my blanket and wiped my tears.

"You can't stay in bed forever," she said.

"Why not?" It made sense to me in that moment.

"What about your life? You must live your life."

"It hurts too much," I replied.

"Life hurts sometimes, *m'ija*, but it also gives," she said. "Life is also full of adventure. You should know that. Remember when you were in Spain and Italy with your friends? What about our time in Maui? Your life is exciting. Why let that go?"

"Life let me down," I said. What was the point of it all, if we all would cease to exist anyway?

I felt her pull the blanket away.

"Now listen to me," she said. "You don't have his illness."

Though I never verbalized it, I had feared I would inherit my father's illness, that I would no longer be myself. I sat up brushing the hair out of my face.

"You are your father's daughter but you are *my* daughter too. Where am I inside you? After all that we've been through, have you ever seen me give up?"

I realized how true her words were. She had always been there and we were nurtured and loved. Mom's spirit was gentle, yet powerful. I realized I was my mother's daughter, and my grandmother's granddaughter. Their best traits were also mine.

"M'ija, you're stronger than you think."

I reached out to her. She held me tight while I trembled and cried. She didn't let me go; instead, she experienced my sorrow with me. I cried until I felt the claws of pain release me and escape through my sobs. With the love in that room, my body

slowly began to come alive. My mother's embrace was like a womb. My deep sobs and tears were the labor, and I was born again as she held me at her bosom. Her words and kindness were the nutrients I needed to open my eyes and live life again. I could continue to feel empty or I could do what she would want: smile, live, love and go on.

"*Qué bueno,*" I swear I heard my grandmother say.

The Other Side of Pain

My mother's visit lifted me, strengthened me. Though some sadness remained, the difference was that the internal embers were being ignited. I began to wean myself off the pharmaceuticals. I did this by intentionally shifting my attention away from the void left by her death and instead relished the wonderful memories of our times together.

I remember seeing on an *Oprah* show about an aging mother who was still grieving the death of her murdered eighteen-year-old daughter. She had held onto the brutal murder for years. Dr. Phil McGraw asked this still-grieving mother why—given the eighteen full years she had with her daughter—she was choosing to focus on just the last moments of her life. How profound, yet how simple, that suggestion was.

I realized I had been doing the same thing.

I was focusing all of my energies on the cruelty, the cancer, grandma's death, instead of her life, her legacy.

With time and maturity, my views on a loved one's death have evolved and are no longer devastating. One friend put it beautifully when she said dying is like when we were born. When we left our mother's womb, we died to one way of being and began a new life. Similarly, when we die, we emerge into a new way of being. Like water, which can freeze, melt or turn into a stream, life is a continuum, with no beginnings or endings. When a loved one transitions, I can miss him or her, but choose to feel deep gratitude for the times we shared and feel blessed with those beautiful memories.

When my ninety-nine-year-old grandfather died four years after my grandmother, I finally grasped the beauty of the Circle of Life. On the day my dear grandpa passed away, a grandson was born. My cousin gave birth to a healthy baby boy. Yes, life does indeed go on. We honor our loved ones' memories and learn from their life lessons. I hope I honor them by how I live my life. Those near and dear to us never disappear forever, because there's still a part of them that lives on in our hearts. Grandma and grandpa left deep heart-prints which will last for years to come.

My emotional wounds slowly began to heal, and I learned new ways to handle setbacks and misfortunes. Instead of viewing crises as solely detrimental, I now see them as nuggets of opportunity. I've learned that from the greatest pains come the greatest joys, healing, understanding and transformation. Just like the caterpillar's amazing transformation into a butterfly, on the other side of painful heartbreaks and tragic losses, life's greatest lessons unfold.

In the process, I have learned more about myself. When I feel upset or pain, I now understand that these are opportunities to practice my tools of spiritual growth. I believe that everything happens for a reason and the serenity prayer helps me to connect with the acceptance, courage and wisdom I need to breathe through the challenges that life throws my way.

Nowadays, I rarely take things for granted. I consider life as precious, with many wonderful surprises and blessings to enjoy. I'm savoring this delicious journey called life, with all of its wonderful ups and downs.

I miss my grandmother. I miss how she loved me. I miss her hearty laugh, her cooking, her cotton pastel-colored housecoat dresses and her pretty slippers. Sometimes, I close my eyes and I can see her short grey curly hair framing her apple cheeks and her beloved smile. I miss her hugs and the touch of her hands, the same hands that cooked thousands of meals and raised five children. She was a wonder woman.

I see clearly what my grandmother instilled in me. I have her love, her grace, her simple tastes and her ability to laugh easily. I will never let her go. I simply have a new relationship with her, as her memories live on in my heart and soul.

My grandmother and mother have taught me a powerful lesson. I learned that before there can be light, there is always darkness. After darkness, there is always light. It is up to us how dark it can get and how bright it can shine.

There is a Native-American tale in which the grandfather tells his grandson, "There is a conflict inside of me and in every one of us. Two wolves live within me. One wolf is jealous, angry, covetous, rude, disrespectful, lazy, unkind, resentful. The other wolf is kind, loving, grateful, compassionate, happy, helpful. They are battling within each of us." The grandson asks, "Which one will win?" The grandfather responds, "The one you feed."

The Life I Feed

I believe we each have a hero's journey. On my own journey so far, I may not have all that I want, but thankfully, I have all that I need. To me, life is about growth and progress, so I honor all of the experiences that have helped me learn more about who I am. Acceptance, compassion and gratitude help me achieve the serenity that I need in my life. I believe that all is happening as it should be; all is in divine order.

I still don't believe in Prince Charming, but I believe in love. I believe in myself. I am my father's daughter; with his aspirations and struggles, I learned courage and compassion. I am my mother's daughter; with her strength in the eye of the storm, I learned to be resilient. I am my grandmother's granddaughter; through her I learned the miracle of unconditional love.

One of my biggest fears is that my father's illness would seize me, too, but I trust in a power greater than me. I choose to live a life of love, learning and resilience, filled with personal joys, victories and adventures. This is the life I feed. Life is not supposed to be easy, but I believe life is worthwhile. In my own path, my work-in-progress, I want to live bold, love deep and experience many wow moments. No regrets. No longing for the past, or for how things once were or should have been. I love my life as it is, with all its blessings and miracles. I believe that heaven is right here, right now.

SUSAN OROSCO is an author and has been a keynote speaker for over twenty years. Her current book *Latino Power: 7 Powers all Latinos Have upon Which to Build an Empire*, was nominated for best self-help book at the Edward J. Olmos International Latino Book Awards. She holds a bachelor's degree in psychology; she is a certified hypnotherapist and has reached the highest level in Toastmasters as DTM. She has worked in sales for over thirty-five years. Susan was born and raised in Toledo, Ohio, and lives in Glendora, California, with her husband Gary, her son Tony, and daughter Melisa.

www.susanorosco.com

The Clearing

"THE MEXICANS STOLE IT!" A VOICE SHOUTED FROM the angry mob. The crowd of men and women waved their fists as they stomped on our freshly mowed front lawn. My father stood firmly at our doorstep defending my twelve-year-old brother from a pack of men who accused him of stealing a neighbor's brand new racing bike. "It's always the Mexicans," another voice called out. "Ever since you moved into this neighborhood, there's been nothing but trouble!"

I was five years old. From the living room window I saw the twisted, red and white faces of the angry mob. They shouted, "Dirty Mexicans! Greasers! Spiks!" They moved closer to the doorstep, waving their fists. My father then pulled his .38 special from his waistband, let off two shots in the air and stood ready to shoot again. The crowd quickly dispersed. I was left standing and forming my new identity: I *am a Mexican, and people don't like us.*

I was born and raised in a little village outside of Toledo, Ohio. We were the only Mexicans in our neighborhood and schools. It was obvious they didn't want us there. There was plenty of prejudice and bullying. My older brothers had to learn how to fight to defend the younger ones.

I was the center of the household, the princess, the picture of innocence. My court consisted of five doting brothers, a beautiful loving mother and a big strong dad—*el jefe* from old Mexico. I felt safe at home until the day my identity took another unexpected turn: I ruined everything by growing breasts and becoming a young woman.

Suddenly, there were no more tea parties with my mother. She turned from sweet to stern. She made me wash dishes and clean my room. She continuously gave me long sermons about the birds and the bees. My handsome brothers, who were once my knights in shining armor, became bodyguards assigned to keep the boys in school away from me. My Papi, my big strong dad who always told me with his special wink how precious I was, stopped looking at me because it was not proper. That was a new slant to my forming identity. I was not proper.

Just like that, my innocence was gone. I was *woman*, the temptation of man. Although it was the late 1960s, the height of the mini-skirt era and sexual power, I was kept covered up. I didn't understand how a short skirt could be interpreted as a desire to control men. Which is what my father would say whenever he saw a woman in one.

I was thirteen and I missed my dad. He became so distant from me. I would ask him questions just to get a conversation out of him, but his answers were trite. It was only when one of my brothers walked into the room and joined the conversation that my father would open up. It hurt to lose him for reasons I didn't understand. I think that's why my heart broke.

The doctors called it rheumatic fever. They operated. The mitral valve and left ventricle of my heart were damaged by infection. At nineteen years old, I was close to death when they flew me to Chicago to receive the advanced medical technology that would save my life.

After the operation I went into and out of a coma. I don't recall much except for my dreams. I remember the first time I had the field dream that was later to become a constant nightly companion. I found myself standing in the middle of an entire field of tall, wild cornstalks. I knew if I could make it to the end of the field, I would find something wonderful. The thick stalks stood in my way. Then a machete appeared in my hand. I knew that each cornstalk stood for an individual pain I'd experienced in my past. I didn't know what to do with the pain or the machete. I just felt surrounded and I trembled.

When I finally woke up, I realized I was in a lot of pain. The left side of my body hurt, especially my chest. My mother explained that the scar under my left breast was not so bad, that a man who truly loved me would not be offended by such a minute flaw. The scar would probably fade away in time anyway, she explained, especially after they removed the stitches. Her words were not as loud as the scar I saw each morning when the nurses changed the dressing. The scar was ugly. I added a new branch to my identity: I was now a monster, Lady Frankenstein.

After three months of intensive care the doctors sent me home with a patched-up heart. I went home a different person. Before my sickness I was full of questions about why my life was so pitiful. After the operation my questions were about why am I still alive. I was determined to find out.

I escaped my death with a ferocious will to live. I wanted to taste life from every angle. I was still a female, a sinful Mexican, a monster, but this time I held life at gunpoint and shouted, "I don't care what you think of me. Show me what you got!" I emerged with a vengeance. I went to extremes. I added a new branch to my identity: angry and rebellious.

I went from being a sick, sheltered, nineteen-year-old girl to a twenty-three-year-old airline stewardess, traveling the whole continental United States. Oh, I had fun, no doubt. Fun determined the quality of life; love had nothing to do with it.

Although the cornfield and machete dream continued to plague my nights, by day I ignored it. I didn't understand it anyway. Instead, I focused on my life filled with parties, one-night stands and flashing neon lights.

I decided to hate the world before it got the chance to hate me first. I thought I was tough and indestructible. I cheated death and grew a heart of steel. I didn't want happiness—I wanted fun. I ran with masses of self-destructive individuals and believed what most people around me believed: I had no control over what happened to me, the world was out to get me, and love was not to be trusted. I did this for five years. The field dream grew more intense. The stalks got taller, wilder, thicker. Sometimes in the dream I couldn't find my machete. It didn't matter. I still didn't know what to do with it.

I met him six years and two months after my heart operation. I was having a bar-hopping night with two other airline attendants. We ended up in a chic night club in Detroit, Michigan. It was rumored Richard Pryor and Pam Creer, the actress, would often hang out there. We were hoping to meet them. We didn't. Instead, I met my Irishman *aka* my hero, my champion which by definition made me his damsel, unfortunately, in distress.

Ralph was chief security in the nightclub. My friends and I were one of the attractions; as airline attendants usually were in those days when they showed up suited-up in uniform. I remember the competition for Ralph's attention that night. There were several young women following him around like groupies, and the men were constantly seeking his approval. He appeared to be an important figure in the bar. He wore a tailored dark-blue suit, with a white shirt and silver cufflinks. He carried a mixed drink in one hand and gestured when he talked. His hair was black, peppered with gray and when he stood next to me, I felt defenseless. When his green eyes met mine, I knew I would belong to him.

My Father All Over Again

Ralph was my first husband. He was tall and strong. He had a powerful chest. He was solid in character, opinionated and firm. He was my father all over again. He would protect me. I knew if anyone tried to hurt me he would beat them; destroy them, kill them. He was my champion. What I later learned is that my deepest fears were not outside myself, they were rooted in my inner demons. And Ralph was no match for them.

We had two children together: Melisa and Anthony. We bought a house in my hometown, Toledo, Ohio. I was happy to be a stay-at-home mom. I believe the four of us were happy, and then things started to change.

After six years of marriage, he hardly spent time at home. He explained he worked all the time. My suspicions, fear of abandonment and insecurity *aka* my inner demons began to rear their ugly heads.

Also, I could no longer deny the smell of perfume or the lipstick stains on his shirts. I screamed, yelled, cried and withdrew. His destruction of me was relentless. I was like my father all over again; he was emotionally leaving me without an explanation.

I knew I couldn't do it again. I couldn't go through what my father had done to me and allow it to reach unbearable heights by letting it repeat itself.

I didn't know what to do. But when I looked at my children, I knew I could lose myself in depression or win myself in revelation. Leaving would be hard, and I would have to do it alone because many people feared him. They did not think I could win against an Irishman. How I could take his two children, bruise his ego and find my freedom was impossible in the eyes of many. But I had a plan.

I went back to live with my parents. My father and Ralph were similar in more than one way. Ralph was a tough guy, all right, but so was my father. And he loved packing a .38 special. Plus he had five sons.

Ralph eventually calmed down, so I let him see the children. He earned it when he agreed with me to have a peaceful divorce for their sake. It took four years but we were finally free of our ten-year marriage.

I found a job as a sales manager for a carpet cleaning company. I rented a brand-new townhouse on Toledo's east side. I was finally on my own. This time I wasn't hurting, or angry, or lost. At least I didn't think so. I was in control of my life for the first time. I thought the pain I carried inside of me was gone. The truth is it was only suppressed. Like a beach ball can be held under water for a very long time until you are exhausted of the effort and let go. It then pops back up to the surface again; so did my pain, and my dream.

George was just my friend. I never felt romantic about him. I met him at mutual friend's party. It was Ralph's weekend with the children, and I felt like getting out so I accepted an invitation to a beer bash. It was fun, and in addition to the beer kegs, George was the life of the party. He was intelligent, interesting and a lot of fun. Our friendship was short lived, because he found a sweet girl and married her. However, he always held a special place in my heart because he was the window that opened when the door to Ralph closed. He introduced me to my artistic side and took me to a place that would change my life forever.

George thought he was a communist, but he wasn't. He was just rebellious. If the world would have turned communist, he would have turned capitalist. He was quite the character. He wore a Green Beret hat and called his friends comrades. He was a political songwriter and musician. It was 1988 and he wanted to be the next Bob Dylan.

I really didn't have an opinion about politics at the time, but I liked George's ability to give a quick well thought-out answer to any question put to him on the subject of politics. George was conflicted on the subject of God. The only thing he had to say about God was written on his bumper sticker above the rear tail light of his lime-green Volkswagen: *God is Love, God is Freedom*. Anything else anybody had to say about God was of no interest to George.

One day George took me out for pizza and then invited me to go to his "room." At first I resisted, thinking he was up to no good with me until he told me he lived at the Collingwood Arts Center in West Side Toledo.

The Arts Center is a Gothic architectural masterpiece that was first built as a convent for the Ursuline Sisters in 1905. Now it was a registered historical site where only artists could live. It was hard to get into the center unless you knew somebody who lived there or who was connected to the administration. I knew none until I met George. I had always wanted to go there. I jumped at the chance.

Once inside, George was in a hurry to take me to his room. I wasn't as eager; instead my eyes just couldn't absorb enough of the grandiosity of the beautiful convent. I wanted to see as much as I could before George captured me as audience to his latest song. The halls were wide and the stairway was grand. Everything was made of cherry wood and smelled like frankincense. There were statues of religious figures like Mother Mary and Saint Francis of Assisi along the hallways and stairway landings.

"What's this?" I asked George as I peered into what looked like a chapel.

"It's a meditation room," George's voice trailed off as a fellow resident artist approached him and they whirled into an intense conversation. I simply went inside and closed the door behind me. I felt a need to be in this room.

I was drawn there and I didn't know why. I didn't think I had anything to meditate on or pray about. Then I had this feeling that if I talked I would be heard. Somebody up there was listening. It was an amazing feeling—actually more like a knowing. So I sat on one of the wooden benches and started talking while staring at a sculpture of Jesus. I was surprised to hear myself begin by blaming God for everything that went wrong in my life. I blamed Him for the prejudice that my family and I endured, for the scar beneath my left breast and for losing the love of my father. I was especially shocked to learn that those old wounds were still bleeding.

I surprised myself at my familiar tone with Him. I scolded Him as though I knew Him, as if it was my right. At that moment I felt a deep connection to the convent, as if I had been a nun at one time and had bequeathed myself to Him only to be betrayed. I wanted His apology or at least an explanation. I cried as I grieved for what should have been mine and never was. I trembled with frustration for the life I had without Him; and then it stopped. I felt that I had been heard. Perhaps even an apology was given, I wasn't sure. But it was closure, and I was at peace. And then I loved Him.

For no apparent reason I suddenly decided I loved Him. I did not love the jealous God or the punishing or destroying God that religion often teaches. That was not the God I was giving myself to at that moment. No, I loved the God that called me to Him, the one who filled my heart with love and joy in that room. I wanted Him. I wanted Him to fill me up completely illuminating any darkness that fostered inside of me.

My wounds were not healed, but I felt a strong sense of direction. I knew exactly what to do. It was time for me to take a good look at my life and a serious look at my field of fears. I was no longer afraid of them. I was ready to call a challenge to myself, to face and overcome the self-limitations and self-doubts. I was ready to pick up the machete and start swinging. I knew this journey was not going to be easy, but I knew I had to begin the process.

George's bumper sticker flashed through my mind: *God is Love, God is Freedom.* Finally, the phrase made sense. I knew I had to clear the way for love and freedom in order to leave despair and distrust far behind me. It was *the clearing* that had to take place so that the real *me* could emerge. It was up to me to prepare for my greatest achievement: the fight for the meaning of my life.

Then I heard a voice in my head say, "Forgiveness brings love."

Learning to Listen

"Forgiveness brings love." That was the first time I ever really noticed the Voice. The second time was when I woke from the field dream one morning with these words echoing in the chambers of my brain. "You want love? Remove all the reasons why you can't have it."

I didn't understand what love had to do with forgiveness. I didn't see the connection. Sure, they were both virtues; but come on, this was real life. According to the Voice, I had to let go of the stuff that hurt me and that included the people. Actually, I really didn't want to do this. I wanted to pick up the machete and cut down all the stuff that stood in my way, but why did I need to forgive?

One day my fears lined up like the planets are predicted to do in 2012. Maybe they lined up to scare me like doomsday, or maybe they lined up so I could cut them down with one single swing of my machete. Victor or victim: the choice would be mine. Did I have the courage?

I was a thirty-five-year-old single mother looking for the perfect man. Instead, I found Richard. I thought he was perfect at the time. He was strong like my dad, dashing like my brothers, and the best part was he was Mexican like me. No more white men; finally my own kind. When I willingly walked into his life, I had no clue I had walked into the deepest level of psychotherapy that existed. The machete should have been up and ready, but it wasn't. When I saw his handsome face, I dropped all my defenses and stood vulnerable. It was as if what had happened in the chapel of the Collingwood Arts Theater had been erased. The level of peace with God I had attained was slipping away. Richard was there to take the place of everything I thought I needed. Even God.

My heart was in Richard's hands. I wanted romance; he gave me romance. I wanted a partner in life; he promised to be my partner for life. I wanted help with my children; he charmed my children. I felt proud and beautiful to stand next to this successful and handsome man. The man I wanted was in the casino business, and he was on his way to Lake Tahoe, Nevada. I wanted to go with him. So, I did.

Tahoe was twenty-two hundred miles away from home. That should have scared me but it didn't. I thought he was the love of my life, but he was more like a cloak of darkness who hid the light. My soul would be challenged.

Oh, don't get me wrong: I was not a victim. To this day, I am grateful for The Richard Experience. He was a sharp contrast to what life is really about, maybe even helpful, like a road sign blaring: "Danger! Wrong way!"

Through his darkness my soul reached for the light. Some of my greatest gifts were the spiritual experiences that came from the inspiring natural surrounding of Lake Tahoe. The trees, the lakes and the mountains became my church.

I needed to find that comfort because I had left my seven-year-old son, Anthony, behind with his father, who did not want me to take him two thousand miles away with a new man who might one day try to take the place of *dad* in our children's lives. He was prepared to fight me with everything he had, and his pockets were deep enough to put up a good legal fight.

I left my son with his father for various reasons. The most compelling was because Anthony wanted to stay. The second was that my older brother convinced me it would be best for him to be with his father during his formative years. Richard encouraged me to leave him behind, too.

Despite what everybody was telling me, I didn't want to leave my son. I was preparing to legally fight Ralph until Anthony took me aside and said, "Mom. It's okay. You can go with Richard. Me and Dad will be fine. Let me stay. I want to stay." It was one of the hardest decisions I ever had to make. It hurt, but I knew he would be okay with his dad. We agreed to certain conditions: Anthony would always have the power to decide which parent he wanted to live with. We also agreed I would have him for three weeks during summer vacation. Anthony also was to have phone privileges to call me any time he wanted.

Anthony, my daughter Melisa and I spent our last night together with a party of cupcakes and lemonade. There were lots of hugs and kisses for Anthony from his two favorite girls. The next morning he sent us off in Richard's Cadillac to Lake Tahoe, Nevada.

The journey into Tahoe was exciting. Melisa, Richard and I were amazed at the sight of the snow-capped mountains and the stillness of the lake. As we traveled further north, we saw the casinos. The streets were filled with colorful flashing lights, inviting you to partake and to test your fortune. Wide-eyed gamblers, dazed with their losses and dazzled with their wins, filled the sidewalks. I didn't see it then, but now I realize the symbolism of how I felt during those days. I was dazed with my unhappiness and dazzled with the promises Richard made. He enticed me to follow the blinking lights to my fortune.

The move to Lake Tahoe was fraught with change and drama, but I tried to keep things as normal as possible for my eleven-year-old, Melisa. Richard and I rented a two-bedroom apartment and decorated her bedroom with her stuffed animals from home and all her dolls. I enrolled her in school and watched her make friends. She held onto me tightly in those days. She was excited too, I thought. Maybe she was petrified. I truly didn't know the difference between these two feelings at the time. I remember we held hands a lot.

Angels in Waiting

We all loved our new apartment and had fun decorating it with our tiny budget. I stayed home while Richard worked. He loved his job at the casino restaurant as food and beverage manager. My favorite room in our new apartment was the kitchen. It was modern but with dark, pinewood cabinets and a pale yellow tile floor. The best part was the window above the sink, where I could see the pine forest behind our building. Looking at the natural strength of the trees, I felt I was in the presence of majesty. The wonder I felt drew me close to something real. *Creations of God*, said the Voice, who often caressed me with gentle words. God was good.

We had a terrific neighbor who lived down the hall from us. Her name was Julie. She gave us a little green foliage plant as a welcome gift. When I told her how beautiful the town was, she said, "Of course it's beautiful. Angels live here." She smiled, and it seemed like the light beam from inside of her gave her a luminous glow. I believed she was going to be my friend.

"Mark Twain said God made Lake Tahoe for His angels, like a private playground." She was pleased to share the information with a newcomer, but there was more to Julie than I could put my finger on. Her smile was delightful but the look in her eyes was serious.

She knew something, and I felt she knew something about me. What could it possibly be? What did my eyes reveal? Could it be that she knew about Richard? Did she hear him come home the night before in his drunken stupor? With that thought, shame flashed through me. I wanted her to like me. I needed a friend like her.

I was needy at that time, no doubt about it. I am sure I was a hard person to be friends with and Julie probably should have done what any other person would have done—stay clear of the likes of me—but she didn't. She stayed close. I look back now and see that she was one of the gang of angels that God had sent to escort me out of hell.

So the Lake Tahoe tango began, and the moves got wild. One night as I was missing my son, I cried myself to sleep and drifted into my dream. I stood in the field of fears again. I was face-to-face with the tall corn stalks. At the other end of the field stood The Promise just as usual, but this time the dream was slightly different.

"Pick up your weapon," the Voice said. So I took the machete in my hand and swung with all my might. Down came two stalks. It was amazing: I had waited a long time for this day. I was actually striking down the stalks. I lifted my machete above my head and swung again. Down came a third one. I felt inspired because I wasn't just whacking at the stalks—I was removing them. It was a clearing and I could see a path.

I felt powerful. It was utterly fulfilling. If this is forgiveness, I thought, I could do this all night. Suddenly I woke from my dream to find Richard on top of me, punching my face.

I could hear my daughter crying, "Stop hitting my mom!" She stood by the door. I reached for my reading lamp on my nightstand and hit him on the head. Twice. He fell beside me on the bed and I pushed him off to the floor. Third strike. Disoriented, but getting up onto his feet, I grabbed my daughter and ran out the door. Down the hall, Julie held open her door. She motioned us in. She called the police, we made a report and, after some time, Melisa and I fell into an exhausted sleep.

The next day we changed the locks to the apartment and a new life began. We didn't get rid of Richard that easily, of course, but the nights got a little better. In my dream, I was chopping down an average of two stalks a night. I was successfully clearing the path that lead to The Promise. Things started to change for me. I was feeling stronger and decided I wanted to see my son. I called and asked if he wanted to come to Lake Tahoe. Of course, he was excited to come and be with us. His father's first reaction was to resist, but I reminded him about our agreement. So, he made the arrangements and soon Anthony was on his way.

His visit was good medicine. I cried, I held, I kissed and I healed. He was so forgiving. He had no feelings of resentment or wrongdoing. He was a happy little guy. I learned, and still learn, calmness by simply being in his presence. I often wonder where in Heaven he came from. My daughter was so happy to see him, too. We were all together, a family again.

In my dream that night, I chopped down three more stalks, heading for the glimmering lights. I was healing. I was emerging. I was beginning to like me.

My son stayed for two weeks out of his summer vacation. He loved Tahoe. The three of us went everywhere together. We hiked into the mountains and enjoyed the lakes. We spent our nights talking and learning so much about each other, it was hard to let him go. I had promised his father I would stick to our rules, knowing that if I kept my end of the bargain, he would let me see him again in the future. Anthony boarded his plane to return to Ohio, and I missed him instantly. Our joy was short-lived. When our taxi dropped us off at our apartment building, Richard was waiting in the parking lot.

Julie was nowhere in sight. I fumbled through my purse for the apartment keys. Richard followed us to the entrance, apologizing all the way. I reminded him that the police patrolled our building more often than usual because of the beating he gave me that frightful night.

"I promise I will never hurt you again," he said.

"No, you won't," I answered as I turned and walked away.

Suddenly, he grabbed my arm. It hurt. "Susan, listen to me," he begged.

Then the resident manager appeared. "Leave, Mr. González," she said. "Or I will call the police."

He dropped my arm, but his eyes stayed on mine as he opened his car door, got in and drove off. I had a terrible feeling that we had not seen the last of Richard.

Still, I moved forward with my life. Julie helped me get a position as a front desk agent at one of the casinos. I loved my job and was good at it. I especially loved not having to depend on Richard for anything. Julie cared for Melisa while I worked, but her help was conditional. She was adamant that I was not to see Richard. I assured her I was done with Richard and not interested in any other man for a while. I decided that when it came to men, I had no idea what I was doing.

Besides, I wanted to spend time with myself. I knew I needed to keep my mind off Richard. Somehow, even though I knew he was bad for me, I still missed him. I wondered why. Was it because I still loved him? Was it because he was the only one I knew from my hometown? Or was it because I missed his car? I chuckled. I was surprised at my thoughts. They were crazy.

I needed a major diversion, so I decided to pursue my interests. I enrolled at Lake Tahoe Community College and began studying Spanish and poetry. I wanted to make myself smart. Surely smart people wouldn't give the time of day to someone like Richard.

What Would Oprah Say?

I made friends at my work and in my classes, but I still felt alone and vulnerable. I tried to be brave and fight the temptation to call Richard. Sure, it sounds crazy, and yes, it was stupid, but there was something comforting about the familiar. The dependable, sick but familiar. Then one day, Oprah spoke.

It was a Wednesday afternoon. I was dusting the living room furniture and occasionally glancing at the television. I noticed Oprah was interviewing an author I liked: Gerald G. Jampolsky, author of the book, *Love Is Letting Go of Fear*.

I sat down and watched. He talked about forgiveness. Oprah then looked into the camera, right at me, and stressed, "Love is forgiveness."

After the show, I dug through some of the old boxes my mom had sent from Ohio and found a cassette of a speech Mr. Jampolsky had recorded years ago. On the tape, he also spoke about forgiveness. I couldn't get enough. At the end, he told a story about a young boy who had approached him and asked, "What does it feel like to be brand new again?"

Mr. Jampolsky said he didn't understand the question at first, until he remembered what he had said in his speech: "With forgiveness, one feels brand new again."

When the tape was over, I was lying spread-eagle on the floor, my arms and legs stretched out in total surrender. Staring at the ceiling, I knew, as I had never known anything before that I wanted to be brand new again.

To do this I had to forgive, and I was willing to do anything to speed up the healing. With each stalk down, the core of my spiritual being emerged some more. I grew stronger and more independent. I especially wanted to be independent of Richard.

Melisa and I were doing well without Richard. We learned the bus schedule in town fairly quickly. South Tahoe was a small community, so taking the bus was a breeze. I especially enjoyed taking the bus to school. My stop was in front of a beautiful little pine forest. I walked through the forest to reach the college. The distance was only about five hundred feet, but the walk was always fully packed with peace, joy and inspiration. I looked forward to being with the pine trees every chance I got.

During my walk on the trail, the forest came alive, one tree at a time, as if each one had a separate personality. Judging from the way they stood, each had a distinct opinion of life. Some grew tall and strong, unbendable. Others were thin and pliable, like the willow. All of them gave off a perfume that was hypnotic to me.

At times, when the wind was just right, they whispered poetry to me. The notion that they whispered to me was as natural as breathing. Except for my mother, I didn't tell anyone about the magic of the pine forest. I kept the joy to myself.

When I was away from the forest, I thought I was crazy. There was no such thing as whispering pine. I wanted to believe in healing, but I didn't understand how. How could I forgive Richard? How was I to forgive the beating he gave me in front of my daughter and the embarrassment of his drunkenness around my neighbors? I couldn't deny that I hated him. I knew it was wrong but I couldn't help it. It seemed my soul would forever host a battleground between my hope and my despair.

Then one day the spirits of the forest surrounded me and gave me a poem. It was a Tuesday. I stayed late in school that day, volunteering to help clean up after our Cinco de Mayo party in Spanish class. As I began my walk back through the forest to my bus stop, I noticed it was darker than usual. I wasn't afraid—not at all. I was only slightly concerned that I might trip over something. I wished I had some light. Then I heard the word *light* and heard myself say:

> Oh, what a light it would be . . .
> if I could be brand new again.

Wow! I thought. I *love this*. Again my mouth opened and I spoke.

> I would rest in your arms . . . knowing
> all my needs You would tend.

I knew I was talking to God. It was a prayer poem, and it was coming fast. I opened my notebook and began to write. It was dark. I couldn't see, but I tried to keep my handwriting as straight as I could and walk at the same time. All I had was the light of the moon and the need to record the moment.

> I would let my soul feed . . . from the
> breasts of Your promises.

Oh, I needed to hear that. I wanted to believe in the Promises at the end of the clearing.

> I would let You bathe me . . .
> in the waters of innocence.

I wanted to be innocent again, to trust and be trusted. I wanted to tell the world, "I am a good girl, really I am!"

Because of my guilt of being a woman, I always felt condemned and believed that only a certain kind of man would find me attractive. Easy prey is the life of a woman who lives in a constant state of apology. I was abuse material.

> I would reach far behind me . . . in search
> of my past . . . and find it gone, along . . .
> with the shadow it cast.

Imagine, I thought, *forgiving myself and being able to reach behind me and feel nothing there but love*. This was a lot to let go of, but I wanted to.

> I would dwell in a raindrop . . . in the ocean
> of time . . . I would play in the now . . .
> and let the now be all mine.

The words were coming faster now. As I wrote feverishly, I knew the poem was a gift not just for me. I needed to pass it on.

> I would take all Your gifts . . .
> and place them into the circle.

I wanted the love in my heart to rise up and take ownership of me and give the world the cornstalks.

> And give back the world . . .
> its meaningless riddle.

Forgive some more, the urging continued. *Let go some more.* I could feel the pain evaporating. I was healing right before my eyes.

> I would mend the mirror I broke . . . as it
> reflected my pain . . . No longer staring at
> me . . . the shattered pieces called man.

Shattered pieces? I wanted to mend. Could I forgive myself for leaving my son behind for my own selfish needs? I resented that I had put my daughter through that terrible night when she saw Richard hitting me. Was self-forgiveness really possible? Was freedom from my own nonsense a destination that could actually be achieved?

> I would fly like an angel . . . dancing about
> . . . free of all anger . . . fear and doubt.

As I walked out of the pine forest I noticed the bright, full moon. At the bus stop I quickly looked down at my notebook to see that my writing was very clear. I remembered that when I had walked into the forest it had been really dark—a black dark. When I left the forest, the moonlight was as bright as though someone had turned on a light switch. I didn't notice at what point it went from dark to light. I remember thinking I may have witnessed a miracle.

> And when the night comes . . . and the
> moonlight glows . . . I will let You wrap
> me . . . in a blanket of miracles.

Landing Forgiveness

Once home, my excited daughter met me at the door. "Tío Nick called," she exclaimed. "He says call him back right away."

My brother lived in Burbank with his wife and two daughters. A thousand images flashed through my mind. Was my family all right? Was he all right? I dialed their number.

"We're fine," he assured me. "It's Mom. She's worried about you. She says you talk to pine trees."

Oh great! I thought I could trust my mom with the secret stories of my enlightenment. "I enjoy nature," I explained to my younger brother.

"She says you don't have real friends, only imaginary ones that live in the forest."

"I have friends!" I shot back, defending myself. "I have friends at work and in school."

"She says your pine trees read poetry to you."

"They don't read it," I exclaimed. "They write it." It was then I realized how ridiculous I must have sounded to him. I was embarrassed.

"Listen, sis, you know I'm only looking out for you. I want to come and get you. I think you could really love Burbank."

"What? Leave Tahoe?" I wasn't sure I was ready to do that, and yet . . . I explained to him that I needed time to think about it.

"Don't take too long to think about it," he said. "I know what Richard did to you. I think you should be with family right now, and so does Mom."

I thought about his offer. I thought about Mom, about Richard, Melisa, school, the pine trees. After four days, I decided to take him up on his offer.

I knew I would miss my special forest, but maybe it wasn't real. Maybe it was my imagination or an illusion. Maybe I needed to be with family; that could help me and Melisa. Maybe it was time to be among the so-called sane.

I waited until my school semester ended. I applied for a job at the Burbank Airport Hilton; they hired me. The hotel was a stone's throw away from Nick's house. Everything was working out like magic. We had a job waiting for us. We had a home waiting. We had family. My daughter was excited. So was I.

Fate took a sudden turn. On the day before my brother Nick was to arrive in Tahoe with a truck, Richard stood outside the apartment building. He held flowers in his hand and wore the saddest look on his face that I had ever seen.

"I know you're leaving," he said. "I know you're going to Burbank."

"How do you know that?"

"Everybody at the casino knows. I don't want you to leave. Forgive me."

Forgive him. There was that word again. I didn't like that word used in the same sentence with Richard, much less coming out of his mouth. However, Mr. Jampolsky had said forgiveness was important in soul healing, important in being "brand new."

"Forgive me," he said again. His eyes began to tear up. He explained that he had changed. At the insistence of his mother, he had searched his soul and realized he had been wrong in how he treated me. It was a new look for him. I had never seen him vulnerable. He reached for me and held me tight. He sobbed and begged some more.

Suddenly I knew what I had to do. So I did what any other red-blooded *chicana tonta* would do. I took him back.

"Are you crazy?" Nick said as he stood next to his furniture moving truck.

He wasn't the only one who thought I had made the wrong decision. Julie was disappointed. "I am very disappointed in you," she said as she walked away.

I should have followed her. I should have said what I wanted to say: "Julie, I have learned to forgive. I'm going to Los Angeles. Richard and I will start a new life. Trust me. All will be well. Trust me." But the words stayed inside me. I was devastated to think I was losing a friend like her. It was the last time I saw her.

To make me more confused and alone, I heard the pine forest whisper, "Trust only what God gives."

All I really trusted at that moment was my need for Richard. I shunned the advice. The pine forest was behind me, and I was looking forward to a brand new life. I was going to be brand new, after all.

That night as I held Richard while he slept, I dreamt that seven unusually tall stalks had grown back in. I stood before them trembling. The machete was nowhere in sight.

Dreams of California

The city of Burbank was beautiful. Many of the homes were Spanish style; some were contemporary. The lawns were beautifully manicured. We drove up to this cute duplex where Nick and his family lived. We lived at the top, a three-bedroom apartment. It was exciting. I couldn't wait to share all this with Richard. He would meet us in two weeks. He got a transfer to a hotel in Long Beach as a food and beverage manager. The hotel provided him with a room. I was glad to hear that, because Nick didn't want him in his house.

I loved my new job at the Burbank Hilton. I made many friends; most of them were in the movie business. They had dreams of becoming actors, writers and directors. I had dreams, too. I wanted my children reunited. I wanted Richard and me to be a couple again. I wanted the white picket fence and the dog in the backyard. I wanted to be brand new. I wanted the good life.

I thought all that rested on Richard, again.

After six weeks, Richard finally settled into his new job in Long Beach, and he was ready for me. He suggested I not bring Melisa on our first weekend together. He had reserved a room for me. At first I thought this was odd. My own room? Then I decided it was like a romance novel, where he would softly knock on my door and ask permission to join me.

I took off work early that Friday. I rented a white, sporty Chevy convertible and drove myself to Long Beach. It was a magnificent five star hotel. "Use the valet," Richard had instructed. "All expenses are paid."

After I unpacked, Richard called to invite me to dinner at the main dining room. We had a lovely seafood dinner with a perfectly matched white wine. We talked about our future together. I was falling in love with Richard again. The candle on the table flickered between us and I was reminded how handsome he was. It was a perfect night until a young woman walked by and said, "Richard, you look good tonight." She winked.

He returned her smile as his eyes followed her out of the dining room doors. "Oh, by the way," he said looking back at me, "I told the general manager you were my sister. That was the only way I could get you a suite for free."

My bite of lobster stopped in the middle of my swallow. I had to push it down to keep from choking. I wasn't sure I had heard him right. "Are you saying that everybody here thinks I'm your sister?"

"Well, not everybody," he said. "Two of my friends in the kitchen know you're my special girl."

I looked at the glass of wine that a moment ago had a bouquet of delight and promise, but was now turning my stomach.

"Oh, don't make that face." He sat back into his chair, annoyed. "I hate when you make that face."

I sat frozen. Shocked and judging from his anger, I must have made the face again.

"You think you're better than me," he sneered as he leaned toward me across the table. "I think I've had enough of your attitude. If we are going to give this another try, you have to change."

"I have to change?" I asked.

"I'm tired of chasing you all over the place. First in Ohio, Tahoe and now here. Damn." His fist lightly hit the table, careful not to draw attention. "Even when I am with you, I have to chase you. I'm tired of competing with your kids, your family and your friends. If you're going to be mine, it's going to be just you and me. We can live like this." He gestured to the luxurious dining room. "Room service, suites and upscale people."

"What about my children?"

"Your kids." He shook his head. "Kids hold people down. That's all they're good for."

I was stunned again. I must have made *the face* again.

"You really think you're all that, don't you?" He sat back in his chair again. "You think you can judge me. I'm the one that puts up with you. It's not the other way around, Susan. I've learned since I've been here that young girls like me. They think I'm Prince Charming. They don't put me through the crap that you're always dishing out. These girls are younger than you, better looking than you. Most of them don't have kids. Now, tell me why I should settle for you?"

"You said you loved me," I said like a dope.

"How can I love you if you don't care about me? You don't care about what I want, Susan." He leaned toward me and lowered his voice. "I'm willing to take you into my life forever if you would just put me before everything in your life rather than putting me last. Besides, do you really have a choice? I know when you were in Tahoe nobody dated you. I kept up with everything you did while we were apart. You couldn't get a man."

"I didn't want a man," I whimpered.

"Nonsense, all women need a man. Admit it. Men don't want women with kids. If you lose me again, you'll be alone for a long time." He calmly sat back in his chair again, taking his wine glass to his lips, waiting for me to beg.

The next thing I remember was running down the hallway and into the elevator. I ran away from him so fast, he was not prepared to run after me. Unlike his promise not to chase me anymore, he was at my hotel suite banging on the door in minutes.

"Open the door, you ungrateful *puta!*" he yelled.

I dialed hotel security.

"You think you can run out on me? You think you can dump me?" He banged the door some more.

"What's the problem, Richard?" a hotel security guard asked. I guess I wasn't the only one to call them.

"I can handle this, guys. You can go," I heard Richard say from the other side of the door.

"I don't think you can, Richard," said another guard as he knocked on my door. "Are you okay in there, miss?"

"I'm okay. Just take him away."

"Do you know this man?"

"Yes," I said. "He's my brother. He's had too much to drink."

"I'm not her brother." I could hear Richard shouting as they walked him to the elevator. "Really, she's my girl. We're just having a discussion. We can work this out."

Once Richard and the guards were gone, I was left with the brutal reality of what had just happened. I was such a fool. How could I have believed he loved me? How could I believe in love at all? I was devastated and I felt a hard shield growing over my heart. *It's to protect me,* I said to myself. It was like a warrior's breast shield. I would not be hurt like this ever again. It shouldn't have happened. How could God betray me like this?

I thought forgiveness was the ultimate spiritual act and that all good things fell into place once I forgave. It wasn't true. I didn't believe it anymore. I wouldn't be fooled again. It was all nonsense: the pine trees, the spiritual walk, the forgiving. Nothing but babble!

I got ready for bed and tried to sleep, despite the desperate ringing of the phone. I wouldn't answer. I had nothing to say. My dreams were gone: the white picket fence, the Lassie-type dog, the swing set in the backyard. All dead.

Richard was right about one thing. I had to change. Something had to give. I didn't want to go on living like this, constantly crying and being beat up inside and out. I hated, but didn't want to hate. I wanted to sleep. I finally did, with no dreams. I left the next morning.

When I got home, the house was empty. Alone, I unpacked my suitcase and got ready to take a long bath, when suddenly I heard a stone hit my bedroom window. That had to be deliberate, I thought. My bedroom window was on the second floor. I carefully looked out the window and saw Richard walking around the house.

How did he know where we lived? How did he know which window was mine? He caught a glimpse of me, smiled and threw another stone. I ran into the hallway so he couldn't see me anymore, when I heard him shout, "I see you. I know you're in there. Come out and play, Susan," he mocked me and threw another stone. I feared he would break a window. How would I explain that to Nick?

He continued to rant and rave and call me names. He blamed me for getting fired from his perfect job. He dared me to come downstairs and face what I deserved. Suddenly, Nick's car pulled up. He sent everybody upstairs and stayed in the front yard to talk to Richard. I watched Richard try to weasel his way out of what Nick had seen with his own eyes. Melisa was up in the bedroom at my side holding me with her tender little arms and asking, "Are you okay, mommy?"

"I hate him," I heard myself say as I looked out the window and watched him lie to Nick.

I could just imagine what he was saying: "We had a little spat. I want a chance to apologize. I love her, Nick. You know how it is."

Nick saw me at the window and motioned with an upward nod, his hands lifted in the air, palms up. The question was obvious. Do you want him? Yes or no? Richard looked up at me with that familiar sad face, but this time I could see the monster behind it. I lifted my head high and shook it—no. My brother smiled. He then turned and, while Richard was in midsentence, Nick punched him in the jaw. The punch left Richard's six-foot frame spread out like fertilizer on the front lawn.

I liked it. I really liked it. It was not forgiveness, but self-defense. Now, *that* I understood. It was my dad all over again with his .38 special, telling the bad men to go away.

The Burbank police arrived and questioned Nick. Richard stood looking up at us, bleeding from the right side of his face. He looked defeated. "*The shattered pieces called man.*" The words pushed out from between my lips.

The police must have come to an agreement with Nick and Richard. Melisa and I watched from the bedroom window as the squad cars and Richard's Cadillac drove away. It was the last time I saw him.

"I hate him," my daughter said. She startled me, because looking at her was like looking in the mirror. Then I heard: "*I will mend the mirror I broke as it reflected my pain.*"

I didn't know what to do, until it dawned on me that she was watching me, like I had watched my father. She was already forming beliefs about herself as she witnessed what happened in our front yard.

"Look at me." I pulled her close. "This is not what men and women do; this is not love. Something went wrong, and sometimes when things go wrong we have to let go. Don't hate Richard. Let's just let him go. We've still got each other."

I held her close as the words *give back the world its meaningless riddle* took on a new meaning.

God Is Love, God Is Freedom

That night I dreamed I had cleared ten tall stalks. I stood further into the field with my machete, which had grown in size and strength. I could see light at the other end of the field. I was clearing my way to sanity. Suddenly I had the urge to look behind me. I saw my daughter at the edge of the field. She was tiny, but ready to chop her first stalk. Her machete was small, but her stalks were tall. She seemed fearless. I was so proud. So proud she would follow me.

For several years after Richard, I didn't get involved with men. I mostly just went out with friends. I didn't trust myself in choosing a man yet. I knew I wanted a good man, a man who truly loved me and liked my children, a man I could trust and rely on. I wanted him to believe in love and to believe in me.

I knew that before I could find a man like that, I needed to be a woman like that. More inner work had to be done, and I was willing to do anything to find more happiness. I was willing to clear more of the fear I felt inside. I held on to George's bumper sticker in my mind. "God is Love. God is Freedom."

With each man I dated, my choices got better. I decided that meant I was getting better.

Seven years passed. Nick moved back to Ohio, but I stayed in Burbank. I was growing stronger inside and I wasn't as afraid anymore. My life was making sense. My son finally came to live with us, and we were a family again. Then one day our family grew by one new member. It was a Wednesday, a very special day.

I was waiting in the parking lot of a mini-mall while my friend, Margaret, shopped. I was taking care of her little boy, Pepo, bouncing him on my lap. I managed to notice a sign outside of a little tavern next to the store: "Karaoke, Weds Nights. At 7 PM."

I wondered why I had never noticed that little tavern before, but promised myself I would one day go in there and listen to the neighborhood karaoke singers. I can't sing worth a lick, but I love to hear the voices of those who can. I continued to bounce Pepo on my lap, when I heard the Voice say loud and clear, "Go inside."

I thought, "Sure, I will go inside one day. I will."

"Go inside," it said again.

"Sure," I responded quietly as Margaret returned to the car and I took her home.

Later that evening after dinner, I heard the Voice again: "Go inside."

I spent the next few minutes arguing with myself. I couldn't go into that tavern alone. I called Margaret. She didn't want to go. I called a few other friends. No luck. I decided to get into my pajamas and find something good on television and get my mind off it. I clicked through the hundreds of cable channels and found nothing to capture my interest.

"I can't go there alone," I argued with myself some more. "What will people say? What if I see one of my neighbors?"

Next thing I knew, however, I was throwing off my pajamas and jumping into jeans and a sweater. I didn't know what to do when I walked into the tavern, so I sat on the first barstool I saw. It was dark inside. "When does the karaoke start?" I asked the barmaid as she served me a beer.

"They're setting up right now. They'll probably begin in a few minutes." She wiped the surface in front of me. I drank my beer, anxious now to walk out of the place. "Okay," I said to the Voice, "you got me here. Now what?"

Then the door flung open. My eyes had adjusted to the dark tavern by this time, and I could see him clearly. He came in with a walk that quickly enchanted me. There was a hop in his step. He was confident. He knew he was well liked. He was dark, handsome and Latino. His hair was black, thick and well groomed. He must have noticed my staring, because he looked to the corner where I hid, hoping no one would see me. He saw me and gave me a wide smile that showed his beautiful white teeth. His lips looked soft under his black mustache. His eyes joined in with the smile.

Love at first sight? No, it wasn't. Somewhere deep inside of me I knew it was not the first time I had seen him. It was like my innermost self already knew him. Not love at first sight. Love at seeing him again. Love at knowing he had waited for me. His name was Gary. He grabbed the microphone and sang with a voice that made my heart dance. I felt like an angel dancing on air. After so much suffering, I felt I had arrived. I was home. Everything that happened to me up to this moment made sense. It was falling together like pieces of a puzzle revealing a picture of an un-shattered me.

Gary and I dated for six months and then got married. He totally accepted and loved my kids. He showered all of us with gifts on our first Christmas together.

Two weeks before that Christmas, however, he built a fire in our fireplace. He then surprised me with a tiny little baby pine tree still in its pot. How had he known? I never told him about the pines. Memories of my pine friends came flooding into my mind. I could smell them. I could hear their whispers. In that moment, I was back in my magical forest. Had they forgiven me? Had Julie forgiven me?

I want to believe they had. I sat in front of the fireplace and felt forgiven. I held my tiny new pine friend on my lap as Gary put a blanket around my shoulders and kissed my tear-stained cheek. "I thought we could plant the tree in the backyard after the holidays," he said. "I thought you would rather have a live pine tree to decorate."

"Thank you." I hugged him as the words *And when the nighttime comes, and the moonlight glows, I will let you wrap me in a blanket of miracles* flowed into my mind.

Come Christmas, my kids made fun of our little pine tree with ornaments hanging from its branches. Today it stands fifteen feet tall, strong and beautiful in our backyard. Gary, too, has that effect on people and things: he nurtures and encourages growth. Both my baby pine and I came into Gary's life small and vulnerable at first, but now, both of us stand tall and certain that we are loved. Forgiveness holds the freedom to love.

Gary, Melisa and Tony are loved, too. They are my family, my miracles. I am overwhelmed with gratitude when I experience the three of them in the same room with me at the same time. There is no denying that my spiritual journey was often tumultuous, but I understand now that the labor of love, like birth, can be painful, and even violent, but worth every tear, every effort and every contraction. I would do it again, gladly. Anything for the love and the life I have now.

I fought for the meaning of my life, and I fought well. I learned to heal my anger, my fear and my hate. I learned that these things did not equal the sum of me. I learned that before a man could love me, I had to love myself. I did this by forgiving, letting go of the way I wanted things to be and accepting them as they were instead. I stopped fighting and started loving.

I also forgave my father's inability to be comfortable with my womanhood. I don't know why he felt the way he did; all I knew is that it had to stop before the shame traveled to my daughter. I forgave my womanhood for him, and that was enough.

I forgave the neighbors who tortured us when I was a child. I understand now, it was only fear. Fear of the unknown. They had never seen brown people before. They didn't understand our ways, our language or our food. Oh, don't get me wrong. What they did was abusive, but in order for me to move forward I had to let my wounds go. I had to let go of trying to change the past and instead look forward to the future. Even more than that, I had to learn to find peace in the present. The only way I knew how to do *all* this was to clear the mess inside of me. With the help of my dreams, the inner voice and my desire to heal, I was able clear the path to my redemption. I know now that when I let go and forgive, I gain the freedom to shout to the world, "I love my life!" And God knows I mean it.

BEL HERNANDEZ CASTILLO is President and CEO of Latin Heat Media, LLC, a multi-media company whose main focus is the production of high quality, profitable content focused on the U.S. Latino market. She is publisher of the only English-language entertainment trade magazine which in 2012 celebrates its twenty-year anniversary. Ms. Hernandez Castillo served on board of the prestigious George Foster Peabody Awards, which honor excellence in radio, television and documentaries, the last year as first Latina Chairperson in the history of the Board. She is currently also executive producer and host of HOLA L.A.! first English-language TV talk show with a Latina POV which airs on KCAL/CBS in Los Angeles.

www.latinheat.com

The Power to Say I Belong

WEAVING HER WAY THROUGH THE ENDLESS ROWS OF towering green and golden cornstalks, through the beautiful hills and valleys surrounding her home in El Rancho de Contreras in Momax, Zacatecas, she was determined to get to the midwife in time to deliver her fourth child. Up ahead, the lull of the river, with the wind whispering through the branches, proved a stark contrast to the piercing contractions accompanying her every step. It was time. As she came to the riverbank, reaching for a tree branch for strength, she let out the last of her labored breaths, then my chrysalis complied, and I inhaled the first of mine. For the briefest moments, we gazed upon each other and we were as one. Then she knew what she had to do, and knew it had to be quick. Lacking the implements of a midwife, using her primeval ingenuity, she reached for the nearest sharp rock. She measured the umbilical cord, four fingers wide, as she had seen the midwife do in her other deliveries; she dragged the rock across the umbilical cord and swiftly severed it. She gently wrapped me up in her *rebozo* and I was ready to embark on my life's journey.

From my mother, my greatest life teacher, I learned that first lesson: in order to survive one needs to be resourceful, resilient and tough.

The Migration and the Search for My Identity

In March 1960, when I was seven years old, my mother finally immigrated us to the United States. I was the youngest of four by her first marriage, which ended when my father was killed, just four months before I was born. Our new family in the U.S. consisted of two older brothers: Manuel and Frank and my only sister, Maria. With my stepfather, my mother had my two younger brothers, Joaquin and Alex who were born in the U.S.A. We lived in a one-bedroom apartment in the predominately Latino neighborhood of Boyle Heights in Los Angeles, California.

On any given Sunday afternoon, I could be found sitting in front of a wooden ledge below our family's apartment, "typing away on my imaginary typewriter at my wooden desk," playing out my secret dream of being a secretary. My mother constantly reminded us that we needed to stay in school so we wouldn't wind up working in a factory, like her. I must have gotten the idea of being a secretary from watching the endless *telenovelas* at home. It wasn't something I learned in school. My elementary school teachers saw my life's potential as a homemaker. I was highly praised when they saw the terrific clay tortillas I made in art class.

By the time I got to Roosevelt High School, I was actually living out my dream. I worked as a clerk/switchboard operator in the principal's office. It was close enough to a secretary in my book—I got to type. I found out fast that being a secretary was not all I had imagined. It turned out to be just a job, a necessity to help with the finances at home.

I was awkward and insecure in high school, as most teenagers are. Having only arrived in the United States nine years earlier, I was still dealing with making myself understood in English. My search for my identity was in overdrive. I got tired of watching *telenovelas*, so I switched to English-language TV. The only thing is, I suddenly disappeared!

There were no Mexicans on English-language TV. Okay, maybe one on *The Real McCoys*. His name was Pepino, the middle-aged ranch hand to "el Señor McCoy," but it was hard to relate to a short, middle-aged man whose name in English translated into "cucumber."

In history class we learned about the Civil War, Betsy Ross and Abraham Lincoln. Every once in a while I caught a glimpse of a few Mexicans. We were always the poor, uneducated peasants or savage Aztecs tearing out someone's heart in the history books. I knew I couldn't possibly be a Betsy Ross and I didn't remember ever having cut out someone's heart. My only option was to think I was a poor peasant, but I rejected that, as well. Where were the heroes in history books or on TV of someone who looked like me? I longed to identify with someone I could look up to. I longed to belong and fit in.

I guess you can say I felt a little out of place in my adopted country. Although I was told I was lucky to be living in the States, I just didn't feel lucky. At home things often turned volatile, with no money and so many mouths to feed. My mother worked two jobs, and our stepfather worked to feed his two boys—he made that clear to us. He also made my sister's and my life unbearable in other ways. We learned to avoid him at every turn.

High school became my solace. I spent as much time as possible at school, away from home. School held many milestones for me. I got my first job, I became politically and socially active and I found my passion for dance, which would be the genesis of what was to become my life. It came in the form of Mexican folk dance.

When it was announced in school that "Mexican folkdance" was now open to all who wanted to take it as an elective, I literally shouted, "This is for me! I'm Mexican!"

Mexican Folk Dance Calls to Me

Mexican folk dance, "Folklórico," called to me with a big *grito*: "¡Ajúa! This is your destiny!" I eagerly obeyed. I had never felt so connected to anything in my sixteen years.

I knew I belonged in the Roosevelt High School Folklórico Group. This music was mine. I could feel my chest swell when I heard "El Jarabe Tapatío," "La Bamba" or "La Negra," as I danced my heart out. The audience's applause fueled the effort and pride of our group as we danced to the *mariachi* and *jarocho* sounds. The reality of just how much I identified with being Mexican was clear. I had found a critical link to who I was.

My love affair with Mexican folk dance allowed me to dream outside the realm of possibilities I was presented with, both at home and at school. At home, I was expected to get a job to help out after graduating from high school. At school, my teachers thought I would make an excellent housewife. "You are so good with your hands, you really should take some more homemaking classes. You're sure to find a good husband when you graduate," the homemaking teacher "advised" me. My counselors never mentioned I could possibly attend college as a dance major. I really had no clue. Had I known I could continue my love affair with Mexican dance and take ballet, modern dance or jazz classes in college, I would have done the *zapateado* all the way to the university.

For the time being, *folklórico* became my passion. It gave me confidence and served as a springboard for me to explore other possibilities.

I met Teresa Quezada and Ruby Cruz in the *folklórico* group. We were considered tall "for being Mexican," we were told by the modeling representatives that came to present a fashion show at our high school. The reps told us we could attend modeling school. When we asked our families, they all had the same reaction: "Qué *modeling school*, ni que la fregada. ¡Mejor pónganse a modelar los trastes!" [What the heck do you mean modeling school. Why don't you model the dishes instead!] It wasn't just the money they didn't have that made them object. Modeling? What kind of job was that for a Mexican? But by then Teresa, Ruby and I were on a glamour mission.

From the little money we earned at our after-school jobs and from collecting soda bottles for recycling (we were ahead of our time by necessity), we were finally able to begin making payments on the $495 it cost to attend the "prestigious" Barbizon School of Modeling. For us it seemed the school was located in an unknown, far-off land, west of Boyle Heights, miles past downtown L.A., further than we had ever ventured out alone: the Wilshire District. It was really only six and a half miles away from our homes, but it was the end of the world, as far as we were concerned. Yet nothing was going to stop us: not lack of money, not our parents, the distance, nothing. So for about six months, as far as our parents knew, we were working late on the nights we took our classes.

At Barbizon we learned to strut our stuff. We developed our catwalk and discovered make-up tips to make our noses appear less "indigenous." We learned to strike fashion poses and how to convert our "barriolicious" look into high couture, which was a little hard to do on our $1.35-an-hour salaries.

However, as exciting as the modeling world was—and even though it did help us with our personal development—it would always come in second for me, as I had found my true calling: dance.

I loved performing with the *folklórico* group, and it showed. By my junior year I had become one of the lead dancers and was chosen to perform at the Dorothy Chandler Pavilion Theater at the world famous Music Center. I'd never seen such a luxurious theater, or so many Anglos in my life! Schools from all over Los Angeles came to perform in a citywide Los Angeles Unified School District arts showcase. I remember feeling belittled when some of the Anglo kids from the Westside schools pointed, whispered and laughed at us. We were as foreign to them as they were to us; the only difference was they felt entitled to ridicule us. But all that was forgotten when we went on stage to perform. The stage was the big equalizer that day as we showed them all the beauty of our world.

After two years, my mother stopped objecting to my *folklórico* passion as long as I kept up with my school work, chores at home and kept contributing to the household finances. She figured this *locura* (insanity) all would end once I got out of high school and got a "real" job. But I had other plans.

I met one of my lifelong friends, Miguel Delgado, through *folklórico*. Miguel was the student body president at Roosevelt High. Teresa and I nagged him to join the *folklórico* because we were tired of only having one male dancer in the group. He finally agreed and found that not only did he enjoy it, he was an exceptionally talented dancer. Graciela Tapia, our dance teacher, recognized his talent, and it wasn't long after that she invited Miguel to join her professional group. That would be the beginning of a career for him that would lead to national recognition and acclaim.

Miguel joining a professional group upped the ante for me. After all, I had already conquered the high school and community stages. I figured it was time that I too went professional.

Since I wasn't offered a spot in Graciela's company, I decided to take her professional dance classes and prove myself to her. Soon I was learning ballet and modern dance and, about a year later, I was finally able to call myself a professional dancer. By then I was traveling up and down the state getting paid to do what I loved, and I had just graduated from high school!

But all good things have to come to an end, especially when there is something better up ahead.

We were out of high school by now and a group of us had gone to see a performance of El Ballet Folklórico de Ema Pulido, one of the premiere dance companies from Mexico. We went backstage and made friends with some of the dancers. They were on a world tour and their next stop was Europe. We became fast friends and official tour guides, taking them around to sightsee in L.A. It was how we learned that some of their dancers would have to return to Mexico and would not be able to continue with the tour. The group was auditioning dancers to replace them. We were asked to audition and—lucky us—Teresa, Miguel and I were selected!

We immediately told the world that we were off to Europe. We were excited, our friends were excited. They even threw us a big going away party.

Then we got word that the tour directors needed to see us.

We arrived at the Montecito Hotel on Franklin Avenue in Hollywood, where the group was staying. The tour was cancelled, they told us. The group was returning to Mexico; however if we still wanted, we were welcome to join them in Acapulco for a gig they were doing there.

We were devastated. All our hopes and plans foiled! How could we face our friends and family? Some had even given us going away gifts. Would we have to give the gifts back?

We left the hotel room stunned and depressed. We walked in silence, down the long hallway, our muted footsteps the only sound on the ragged carpet. We stepped into the cold steel elevator, forgetting to even push the floor button. We looked at each other, speechless. As the door began to close, we burst into smiles and simultaneously shouted, "We're going to Mexico!"

Neither Mexican nor American. I'm Chicana.

We left for Mexico two weeks before Christmas. As far as our families knew, we already had the job. We didn't dare tell them we didn't know where we would be staying or how long our money would last, or that we didn't really have a job, only the promise of one.

On a slightly overcast day that winter of 1974, Miguel, Teresa and I boarded the Greyhound bus in grand style (thanks to the tips we learned at Barbizon). We excitedly waved goodbye to our respective family members. There were tears (on their part, not ours) as they wished us well and sent us off to our mother country.

After a bumpy, four-day bus ride, we arrived in Acapulco only to find that the *folklórico* group had already filled our positions! We were disappointed, but what could we do? We had no binding contract. Besides, we weren't going to let the fact that we were in a world-renowned vacation resort go to waste.

We quickly found a room to rent and proceeded to living the tourist life. We spent our days on the beach and our nights at the trendiest Acapulco nightclubs, thanks to our dancer friends.

The three of us grew closer and bonded in a way only friends who are faced with adversity can. Our naiveté and sense of adventure kicked in. Not only did we find a way to survive, we even relished the adventure.

Christmas came and went, and we spent it in our rented room. It was the leanest Christmas I can remember. My only gift was a handmade Christmas card of the three wise men drawn by Teresa. I still have it to this day. Despite the circumstances, we laughed and enjoyed our Acapulco adventure, confident things would work out.

However, a month later—with money running out and with our meals now consisting of a dozen tortillas and a handful of jalapeños split three ways—we knew it was time to move on.

We finally hitched a ride back to Mexico City, *la capital*, and back to reality.

With no job in sight, we ended up in the home of Miguel's aunt, who at first received us with open arms, but after about six months the whole family was ready to kick us out, and rightfully so.

By then, Miguel decided it was time to go back home. Teresa and I continued our *folklórico* dreams and studies at the world renowned Ballet Folklórico de Amalia Hernández. When we couldn't hold out any longer for a spot with Amalia's group, we took a job at the Ballet Folklórico de Javier De León at Plaza Santa Cecilia, performing for tourists. We were enjoying our new professional dancing lives and thriving in our new cosmopolitan city. By that time, we were feeling like *chilangas*, a term used to describe Mexico City natives. But boy, was I in for a reality check.

Chicano Power!

In Mexico, I felt at home; I felt I belonged. I'd never felt like that growing up in Boyle Heights, where I was made to feel that Americans were better than Mexicans. But now here I was, a Mexican among Mexicans. Or so I thought. My real *chilanga* friends in Mexico saw it quite differently. They were shocked when I spoke Spanish: "*Me voy ir en el carro a la marketa y me voy a parquear en el lot.*" ¿Que qué? They would laugh. They called me a *pocha*, a negative termed used to identify a Mexican who has grown up in the United States. Every time I mispronounced a word, they were sure to remind me that it was incorrect. They said it in a nice way; after all, they liked hanging around with us *pochas*. But after a while, I was getting the sense that I wasn't one of them, that I wasn't as Mexican as I thought I was.

It was in Mexico that I came to the realization that I was neither Mexican nor American. I was Chicana. I had first heard that term while still in high school during my so-called radical period, when I took part in the student walkouts. "Chicano Power!" "Chicano Power!" I yelled, along with two hundred other students as we made the trek from Roosevelt High School to the Los Angeles Unified School District offices. We were protesting the deplorable conditions in the schools and the "advice" of our counselors, who pushed us to go into auto shop or homemaking instead of college.

However, I had never truly grasped the meaning of the word *Chicano*. Now it made sense. U.S. Latinos faced issues our Mexican counterparts didn't have. Mexicans knew who they were. They turned on the TV and saw lawyers, presidents and doctors who looked and spoke like them. They were taught their rich history, learning about their Mexican heroes. On the other hand, living in our adopted country, we could only identify with the poor peasants in the U.S. history books or the current Latino faces on English-language TV. You know the ones: the bandits, maids, gangbangers and illegal aliens.

After two years in Mexico, this Chicana decided it was time to go home. Teresa stayed in Mexico for eighteen more years, moving on to a modeling career, which took her all over the world.

Meanwhile Miguel, who had returned home a year and a half earlier, was busy in Boyle Heights starting his own dance company, Teatro Mexicano de Danza/Mexican Dance Theater. Upon my return, he asked me to join him as his assistant director. I was honored to work with him again.

The Miguel Delgado Effect

Miguel's philosophy on choreography was to focus on the dance theater of the U.S. Latino experience. In addition to the traditional folk dances of Mexico, our dance company performed original pieces set to the music of well-known Latino musical artists or classical music composers like Silvestre Revueltas, or popular groups like Tierra or Los Lobos. Miguel also choreographed numbers to the music of the 1940s and 1950s, infused with the Latino/Chicano life experience. His dance pieces delved into the historical context of the times. He was a true pioneer of Mexican and U.S. Latino dance folklore.

It was about this time that *Zoot Suit*, a play written by Luis Valdez, founder of El Teatro Campesino, was being cast at the Mark Taper Forum of the Music Center in Los Angeles. They needed an assistant choreographer and liked what Miguel was doing, so off to the theater Miguel went. The play became a phenomenon, playing to packed houses and receiving rave reviews. It became the first L.A. hit play based on Latinos to go off to Broadway. When they needed to recast the L.A. production, upon Miguel's urging, I auditioned for the role of understudy for one of the dancers and was cast in my first professional union stage play.

Every now and then I would marvel at the fact that only eight years earlier I had been at the Music Center's Dorothy Chandler Pavillion, performing and being snickered at by some of the students. Now here I was at another Music Center theater production, performing in a hit play. I was glad I hadn't let those remarks deter me from pursuing my dance dreams. I had learned my mother's lesson of being resilient. Had I not, I wouldn't have found myself part of a hit play, receiving standing ovations from audiences that included John Travolta, California Governor Jerry Brown, Anthony Quinn, Robert Wagner, Natalie Wood, Erik Estrada, singer Linda Ronstadt, friends, family, Latinos and non-Latinos.

I also met the love of my life while doing the play. Enrique Castillo, the man who would become my husband five years later, played the lead character of Henry Reyna in *Zoot Suit*. They say opposites attract, and in this case we couldn't have been more different. He was the strong, silent type. I, on the other hand, had not met a party I didn't love. It was a challenge, but we made it work.

Zoot Suit ran for a whole year and when it was over, I had found my new career: acting. I realized an opportunity to be in a hit play like Zoot Suit was a rarity, so to continue in my newfound profession, I needed training. I immediately began playing catch-up with acting and voice lessons, commercial classes, cold-reading classes and of course the ever-present dance lessons, which I did have a leg up on.

Up until this point, the only Latino actors I knew of were the ones I saw in the Spanish-language *telenovelas*. Rarely seeing Latinos on English-language TV led me to believe that Latinos weren't good enough to be there.

Having to audition for a roomful of Anglo producers and competing alongside other Anglos was a daunting experience. I often convinced myself that I wasn't going to get the role because they were better than me. It took many nerve-racking auditions to realize that not all Anglos were talented. Realizing that I was just as talented as the *gringos* gave me the affirmation and encouragement I needed to continue.

Stand Up for Your Rights

In the early 1980s, there were just a handful of Latinos in Hollywood. Most of us had been in Zoot Suit. Many of us continued our friendship off the stage. We were like a family that included Lupe Ontiveros, Edward James Olmos, Tony Plana, Dyana Ortelli, Evelina Fernández, Sal López, Cris Franco, my husband, Enrique and, most all the other Latinos in the cast, who continue in the business to this day, either as actors, writers, directors and/or producers. We got together for birthdays and anniversaries, attended each other's baby showers, celebrated our career successes or cried on each other's shoulders about our disappointments.

In spite of the lack of good roles, most of the members of our core group made a good living, building up our resumes doing television, film, commercials and theater. However, we tired of only being allowed to audition for the same stereotypical roles.

We were a vocal group and we vowed to try to change things. We were always brainstorming, planning and organizing about what we could do to bring about change. We wanted the right to audition for the lead role of a lawyer, teacher, even secretary. But Hollywood wrote very few of those roles for Latinos at that time.

We all became quite resourceful and had to find a way not only to survive but to fight for what we felt was right. We lobbied the two actors' guilds, attending en masse countless meetings to voice our opinions and propose solutions. Management listened and said they understood and promised to do something about it. They never did.

In 1988, we met with Mario Obledo, then president of LULAC (League of United Latino American Citizens), a Latino advocacy organization that occasionally lobbied Hollywood for better Latino representation. In the end we were told that although our dilemma was an important one, we needed to understand that LULAC had "more important things" to address such as health, education, economic attainment and civil rights.

We understood all right. We were on our own.

It was 1992 and things hadn't changed all that much. In the interim since *Zoot Suit* had closed, Luis Valdez had gone on to direct *La Bamba*, the highest grossing Latino-themed film in the history of Hollywood at the time. Now he was working with New Line Cinema to write and direct a movie about world-renown Mexican artist and activist, Frida Kahlo. Our group was thrilled, especially the Latinas, because finally, here was a positive role we could all audition for.

Well, we could have, but New Line Cinema, the production company, was not having any of that. After auditioning only two Latina actresses, Newline declared that they couldn't find a "box office Latina" to play the role of Frida. We felt betrayed and excluded. Here was a role about one of the most vocal proponents of Mexican culture of her time and Latinas weren't even being allowed to audition? Frida must have been rolling over in her grave. Instead, they decided Laura San Giacomo was the box office name they needed. Laura San Giacomo who? She's known now, but at that time she was an actress with minimal credits. Well, that was the last straw.

"I don't know about you, but I am protesting this, even if I have to do it alone!" The words of Dyana Ortelli, a fellow Zoot Suiter, echoed in the conference room where she had called a meeting that was attended by almost every single Latino actor in Hollywood.

She didn't have to do it alone. The women coalesced and organized a protest in front of New Line Cinema. We raised the money, sent out press releases, booked the hotel to hold a press conference and made our picket signs. More than thirty national and international, Spanish- and English-language media, outlets covered the protest.

More than two hundred of us, including my two- and thirteen-year-old daughters, marched in front of New Line Cinema dressed up as Frida, uni-brow and all, chanting, "If Frida was alive today, would you let her audition?" We also had the support of actors like Edward James Olmos, Esai Morales (who played Bob Morales—Ritchie Valens' brother—in La Bamba) and several others who showed up among the protesters.

In the end, New Line canceled the movie and no one got the role. In retrospect, we were glad the movie didn't get made at that time because it cleared the way for Salma Hayek's Oscar-winning *Frida*, released in 2005, which she produced and starred in as Frida Kahlo.

After this experience I realized we could stand up for what we believed and get results.

New Line Cinema's reason for hiring San Giacomo was that there was no "recognizable" Latino talent. We were the talent and we knew where to find it—it was *us*. We realized there needed to be a forum to highlight the Latino talent in Hollywood and address the issues that concerned our community or the lack of roles, or stereotypical roles would continue for Latinos in Hollywood. In our quest to demand a right to the process, we found that we had the power to effect change by providing insight to an industry that had long ignored our talent.

Hollywood Takes Notice

In 1992 *Latin Heat*, an entertainment trade publication focusing on Latino talent, was born. In the beginning, it was published through the efforts of the core group that had participated in the New Line protest. However, since actors comprised the majority in this group, they soon turned their focus on their careers and the day-to-day tasks of publishing fell on a friend and fellow actor, Loyda Ramos, and me. We both continued acting and devoted every extra minute to publishing the magazine.

Two years later, when Loyda also left to focus on her career, I decided to continue on my own and was later joined by Elia Esparza. I was grateful that Loyda had helped set the foundation for the magazine. She showed me that we could tackle any issue and approach anyone in the business, no matter how high up we thought they were, and that they would respond. This realization gave me a belief in myself that enabled me to work on a different level. I was empowered, knowing that the magazine wasn't just about me; it was about changing minds and creating a community: our Latino Hollywood community.

At this juncture, I had been happily married for eight years and had a three-year-old daughter, Karina. From my husband's first marriage, we had a thirteen-year-old daughter, Alma, and a twenty-year-old son, Sol. My acting career was at its pinnacle. I had just shot the pilot episode of *Beverly Hills 90210*, in which I played a teacher! It was one of the few non-stereotypical roles I'd been cast in, and this time it was to be a recurring role. However, my life's calling was tugging at my sleeve.

The impact *Latin Heat* was having on the industry was growing exponentially, positively affecting the talent that was being covered in our bi-monthly publication. Hollywood began to take notice. The magazine needed my full-time attention now.

My world as I had known it up to then, slowly began to disappear. I no longer had time to go on auditions and, most surprisingly, I didn't want to go. I was happier to stay and prepare the next issue.

My newfound passion would eventually push aside all that I used to be to make way for all I would eventually become. I was driven as I hadn't been since my *folklórico* days. This is where I belonged. It felt right.

As a dancer and actress, my priority had been me. With publishing I was treading unfamiliar waters and it meant I needed to acquire a whole new set of skills. My only prior publishing experience consisted of working as an assistant to an advertising director at a Spanish-language newspaper, but I needed to know more. A mentor of mine, Kirk Whisler, who heads the Latino Print Network, had been keeping tabs on the progress of *Latin Heat*, and with his recommendation, I received a scholarship to attend the Stanford Professional Publishing Course at Stanford University.

Never being one to shy away from hard work and the challenge of learning new things, I dove in. If my mother could immigrate with four of her children and raise six kids working two to three jobs at once—without the benefit of speaking English or having more than a fourth-grade education—I could surely handle a new career in publishing.

At the Stanford course, I met the former publisher of *Vibe* magazine. His new publishing company, Vanguard Media, was looking to get into the Latino market. I gave him my business plan and before I knew it, contracts were on the table. I was ecstatic. Finally, we were going to get the cash infusion that would allow us to print monthly. But I had to give up 80 percent ownership. I hesitated. All I could think was that I would be giving up control of the magazine. Although I would stay on as publisher, I felt the mission of the magazine would be compromised. More importantly, if I gave up 80 percent ownership, *Latin Heat* would no longer be Latino owned, and that was important to my husband and me. We turned it down.

We continued without funding and focused on trying to effect change through the power of the written word on a shoestring budget. We were succeeding. We were becoming a voice for a sector of the entertainment community that had long been gagged. I mostly enjoyed the fact that our editorial content was stimulating dialog on a national level. We were gathering an impressive readership that consisted of high-profile entertainment professionals, both Latino and non-Latino.

We were being featured and quoted in local and national magazines, such as *Latina*, *Vogue*, *Hispanic Business*, *Hollywood Reporter*, *Movie Maker Magazine*, *Hispanic Magazine* and on local and national television and radio shows. I was invited to speak about Latinos in the industry on panels across the country at universities, conferences and film festivals, even at the Smithsonian in Washington, D.C. This helped establish *Latin Heat* as a publication with a strong voice and mission.

The positive response to *Latin Heat* validated our existence. Drawing on my past political and social consciousness awakenings ignited during high school, I was able to identify and convey the *Latin Heat* mission more clearly. It was about access and positive images.

On a personal level, being a publisher had given me more of a sense of validation, much like what I experienced when I discovered *folklórico*. The relationships established during my acting career helped *Latin Heat* gain access to the now rising Latino stars for interviews and event participation.

Living and Breathing *Latin Heat*

While my relationship with my computer and Hollywood grew stronger than ever, my relationship with my family was on a crash course. I immersed myself in the work, not realizing how much time I was taking away from my family. My focus shifted from my family to making sure the next issue was printed and distributed every other month.

Work could go 24/7. I felt like a wind-up toy that never unwound. Getting together with friends was a luxury. I spent most of my time in the office or in my car driving to and from Burbank, where our offices were located. I didn't allow myself time to think; life was too busy for that.

I was riding a humongous, thirty-foot wave and I was determined to ride it to the end, but what that end would be, I never stopped to think. What I did know was, I had be tough and work hard to survive, even if I had to do it alone. My pride prevented me from reaching out for help. My self-doubt prevented me from stopping to think things through. I felt if I stopped I might find out that I didn't have the necessary skills to pull this off!

I had always been proud of my multi-tasking skills, but they seemed to be collapsing under the weight of the overwhelming workload. I was trying to apply my mother's winning formula of being resourceful, resilient and tough, but I wasn't getting the results I needed. To make matters worse, I couldn't do a good job at home and still do a kick ass job at work growing the business.

The magazine began to take over my life as my family began to lose out. Yet, I couldn't understand why they didn't see that it needed to be this way.

I tried being resourceful. I would rush home in hopes of being on time to read my daughter a bedtime story. I would get into bed with her, trying to make up in thirty minutes for being away all day. I hoped that by the end of the story she would be fast asleep and I could feel good that I had done my motherly duties for the day. However, almost invariably, as I was sneaking out of the room, she would open her eyes and say, "Mommy, where are you going"? I would lie back down with her and cuddle some more, all the while thinking of all the things I needed to get done.

When I did get to bed, about 2:00 or 3:00 a.m., I had dreams of budgets, office rentals, ad sales, hiring and managing employees. I would bolt up in the middle of the night, startled that I might have forgotten to do something and vowing to remember when I woke up. My first waking thoughts were always of the office and about the work ahead of me.

Latin Heat had always been high on content but low on funds. Making a profit was a luxury we didn't have, no matter how resourceful we were. There were many times when my husband and I had to "invest" our personal monies to keep *Latin Heat* afloat, which created stress and tension in our marriage. My obsession with the magazine was pushing us apart.

Almost from the day we met, my husband and I spent most of our time together. We have always been best friends. We have the same goals, interests and family values, and we truly enjoy each other's company. Our lifestyles as actors afforded us the luxury of spending more time together than the usual couple. So as that lifestyle diminished, the resentment began. We rarely saw each other. When we did, we often argued about my time away or finances. Good memories during this time were hard to come by, leaving room for more bittersweet ones.

There was the time I rushed home from the office one Christmas Eve. Running late, I hurriedly wrapped last-minute gifts and began preparing dinner for the family and invited guests. My husband announced that he wanted to take pictures with his family, calling each of his children one by one. I waited to hear him call my name. When it didn't come, my heart fell. My brother-in-law must have seen the sadness in my eyes because he jumped in and said "and Bel" and pulled me into the picture.

Maybe it was my guilt that made me feel I couldn't just jump in and join without being asked. I just remember that as I posed for the picture with a smile on my face, I cried inside, and when the picture was developed, I took it and hid that painful moment from everyone.

Although *Latin Heat* was an intruder in my family life, I couldn't leave it. I needed it and it needed me. I would often ask myself how I could be such a bad wife and mother? Other times I rebelled. Why didn't I have the right to focus all the time I needed on this career? Why couldn't my family understand that it was important? This situation made it impossible for me to savor the good times.

In 1997, the Hispanic Public Relations Association recognized me with the Premio Award. I was invited to the luncheon to pick up the award. I couldn't bring myself to invite my husband to go with me. How could I tell him my neglect of my family had resulted in my receiving an award?

It was my husband's validation that mattered to me most. I needed my husband to reassure me that what I was doing was good and important. I needed it to fight my insecurity.

Enrique has always been supportive of whatever I wanted to do. He is not the typical macho man who stands in the way of what I want to do. He has never second-guessed what I did or how I did it. I did that quite well by myself. But I wanted him to tell me that taking time from the family and not finding a balance between family and career was all right. I wanted him to take on all the family obligations so I could focus on the magazine.

The times he did reassure me, I found myself wondering if he really meant it, because deep down inside I knew what I was doing wasn't right. In retrospect, I realize I was playing the victim, sabotaging myself, setting myself up for failure.

However, that needy person did not show up at *Latin Heat*. At work, I was a rock because I needed to be in charge. I needed to be in control. I had to be the tough one; work the hardest, get the job done. I mentored young men and women. I often sat with staff, answered questions for our readers or people who'd call the office randomly; I was taking care of their needs before my family's. It made me feel good to be able to help.

I wasn't thinking straight. My mind was crashing under the strain of dealing with a business growth spurt that could not be financially sustained.

For the most part I kept the business financial problems to myself. My husband had his own career to concentrate on, I reasoned. I usually excluded him from any decisions at *Latin Heat*. It was only when crises at the magazine would arise that I would have to tell him that I needed his help.

Finally, my world came crashing down. My inability to sustain financial stability for *Latin Heat* finally forced me to lay off most of the staff and close the office. I told no one, other than close family and friends.

Pushing Forward

Alone, I closed up the *Latin Heat* offices after six years at that location. Alone, I packed up all the struggles, successes, triumphs and angst, putting them into big and small boxes along with the paperwork, copies of the publication and the numerous awards and commendations we had received over the years. With each trip I made up and down the stairway I had walked up so eagerly in the past, I cried a few more tears.

Having to close down the *Latin Heat* doors was probably one of the best things that could have happened at that point in time. I got so blinded with the need to be successful that I was losing my family and I realized that was not a price I was willing to pay.

I set up my home office and little by little I began sharing more of the business with my husband. Although I was still working long hours on the magazine and actively seeking investors, I was home, in the next room and more accessible.

Enrique and I were becoming true business partners. More and more of the business decisions were being shared. In addition, I was able to bring some of what I had learned to help with some of Enrique's film projects, which we were now producing. It was a tough transition but it was the right move. However, the move did not come without its difficulties.

I didn't realize it at that time, but I fell into a deep depression that lasted a couple of years. It manifested itself with bouts of angry outbursts in public. A visit to the bank could find me screaming at the top of my lungs with expletives if things didn't go my way. There were also spontaneous crying spells at the doctor's office, with friends and in business meetings. For once I couldn't tough it out. I needed a release to be able to start again, because giving up was not an option. My survival instincts kicked in, and somehow I knew that I would get through this tough time.

Knowing Who You Are Lands You on Your Feet

I was able to keep *Latin Heat* moving forward. I was even able to find an investor and we began back in earnest. Although we no longer print on a regular basis, *Latin Heat* now lives on the internet, where more and more magazines are taking their editorial. We are also now producing for film and TV.

Returning home and dedicating more time to my family helped me move from the brink of divorce to rebuilding a relationship with my husband. It was hard and took several years but the effort worked. We joyfully celebrated our twenty-eighth wedding anniversary in 2012.

As for my youngest daughter, she tells me now that she remembered my being gone so much and that is why at bedtime she didn't want me to leave her bed. I was glad that my decision also allowed me to guide her through the awkward teenage years. Spending her share of time in the *Latin Heat* offices while growing up gave her an insight into all the work that we did. Now she is part of the *Latin Heat* team as an on-camera host and also works behind the scenes on production. She has decided she will pursue an acting career.

Where did I get the notion that a woman can do it all with no complications? Maybe it was that darn Enjoli TV commercial I grew up watching.

I went like this "I can bring home the bacon, fry it up in a pan and never let you forget you're a man. Cuz I'm a Woman."

I had seen that perfume commercial in the 1980s and bought into it. Why couldn't I run a business, raise a family, make my husband happy, keep a spotless home and look like a million dollars all at the same time? There were women who could do it all—I had seen them in the movies and on TV! I wanted to be that superwoman. I found out that I couldn't be and that I needed to make concessions.

Know Who You Are

My work at *Latin Heat* opened doors for me I never dreamed I could walk through. One of those was serving on the board of the prestigious George Foster Peabody Awards, which honors excellence in electronic media in the United States and internationally. I was on the board for six years, the last one as the first Latina chairperson in its history. In 2008, my last year as chairperson, I addressed an audience of nine hundred at the Waldorf Astoria in New York at the Peabody Awards luncheon. Among the audience members there to pick up their awards were CNN's Christiane Amanpour, Bob Woodruff, Bob Weinstein, Steve Carell, Heidi Klum, the whole cast of *Mad Men* and Tina Fey. I took the opportunity to speak about something close to my heart: the importance of diversity and positive images.

It was the lack of positive images and the search for my identity that put me on the trajectory of self-awareness and self-image, beginning with *folklórico*. Those needs shaped what I believe in and what I continue to believe and fight for. All children need to know that they matter and they need to see themselves and their culture reflected in the media.

Once you know who you are, you will always land on your feet. It doesn't matter that you stumble along the way.

I look back on the early years of *Latin Heat* with great satisfaction. I see my personal growth, from the girl who felt inadequate and lacked confidence to the woman I am now, and I smile. I was part of a historic publication and movement that helped shine a light on the need for positive images of Latinos in Hollywood—the images I so desperately searched for when I was growing up.

Yes, life is a road full of hills and valleys. But if you hang tough, are resourceful and resilient, you will inevitably climb out of the valleys, build on the knowledge of your journey and be able to shout "I love my life!" and mean it!

JOANNA ILIZALITURRI DÍAZ is a writer, playwright, project strategist coach and a leader within the healthcare industry. She holds bachelor's degrees in business administration and business management. Her creative works have been featured in *Ride to the East Side* CASA 0101 theater productions and she was the co-producer of the *8 Ways to Say I Love My Life* theatrical production. Her business career includes partnering with organizations to develop small-to-medium businesses and help them strategize their business plans. She has held officer roles within nonprofit organizations, including Toastmasters International.

¿Qué te dice tu corazón?

OF ALL THE VIRTUES I HAVE LEARNED IN MY LIFETIME thus far, the phrase "Follow your Heart" venerates them in a way that the experiences which lead to this point in my life only could.

The phrase is a culmination of all the lessons that have made me a stronger person. Some lessons harshly learned yet they strengthen the shield that protects my heart and others have heightened the awareness to my intuition, sharpening my mind to find wisdom and take on the challenges that lie ahead. I, like the guiding forces of the women in my life who came before me, have faced many trials and tribulations: learning the virtues that culminate the phrase would beg to question, "*¿Qué te dice tu corazón?*" Like my mother, mommy, mom, I too learned how to manifest my heart's desires, and it wasn't easy.

Mother crossed the border at Mexicali into California in 1973 with my two-year-old brother in one hand and a very pregnant belly. Against my father's will, she planned on having me in the good old United States, in search of a better life. What she never imagined was that in pursuing her dream with all her enthusiasm, tenacious nature and love of life, she would place our family at risk. Our lives would be torn apart. Our home and everything we knew to be safe and sure and right disappeared in the blink of an eye. Our world shattered when we became victims of government agencies that took us away from her. My brother and I would be alone and at the mercy of strangers.

I was only five years old when we lived this frightening experience. My own strength and spirit took root, however, and I saw the world with wiser eyes.

The Move

A few months after my birth, mother headed back to Mexicali with a birth certificate, a diaper bag, Manny and me. Even though we were surrounded by my loving tías and Papi, Mother had bigger dreams that she thought she could only make real in the United States. For four years she often lovingly encouraged my father, a mellow and gentle man, to move us to the United States. However, his roots were in Mexicali. His parents and eleven siblings had been born and raised there. He was torn between staying there and pursuing his wife's desire to move to the United States.

Mother wouldn't wait. She had an urgency to act on her dream. She left us with Papi a number of times to take short trips to the States to take care of paperwork. What he didn't know was that during her visits, she was working and saving money with the intention of making the United States our new home.

One day she decided to leave Mexicali for good, whether Papi liked it or not. Mommy packed our clothes and in the midst of darkness, she, Manny and I drove across the border to begin our new life. Papi stayed in Mexicali. I didn't get a chance to say goodbye to my tías or Papi.

We were suddenly in the United States.

A couple of months later, Papi joined us and tried to make it work. Although I was a child, I sensed his anger, sadness and desperation. Living in America with *los gringos*, the white folks, was difficult for him. Papi realized that mother was staying and nothing would convince her to return to Mexicali.

"*¿Estás loco?*" she exclaimed, when my father insisted on taking us back.

"*Por los niños,*" he'd persist. For the kids.

My mother didn't budge. My father returned to Mexicali without us.

In our new life in Orange County, California, we stayed with friends and relatives. Those were hard times. We slept on the floor in sleeping bags. Mommy worked long hours, and Manny and I were left with people we barely knew.

When Mommy finally was able to afford an apartment, I was excited to roam freely throughout the house and play hide-and-seek again. The next-door neighbor was our babysitter while Mommy went to work.

Routinely at five o'clock in the evening she returned from work. We were excited to see her. She gave us big hugs and kisses. We were happy, just the three of us living in our own place.

Being a single mother was difficult. As a piecework seamstress, her job didn't pay well. The little money she made was for necessities and not much more. At one point, Mommy could no longer afford to pay the babysitter. It was summer and school was out. She had no choice but to leave us in the apartment, alone. She still prepared the meals and set the rules.

"Play inside, be as quiet as you can. Remember, strangers are watching." She held her index finger to her lips. "Shhhh, okay? Don't open the door or look out the window." A big hug and kiss, and away she went into the cold world she so valiantly protected us from.

The first couple of days Manny and I were home alone, we played quietly inside the apartment. We waited to hear Mommy put the key in the keyhole and tug at the knob, our signal that she was home.

"Mommy!" Manny and I jumped, giggled and greeted her with hugs and kisses.

During the next couple of weeks, the babysitter neighbor approached Mommy about taking care of us. She needed the money as much as Mommy needed it to pay the bills. She reminded Mommy about the dangers of leaving us alone. Two weeks passed.

Mommy worked with large industrial sewing machines that sewed leather wallets and belts. Her fingers were often covered with Band-Aids. Sometimes she would lose her concentration just thinking about us and sew through her fingers with the machine.

One day, after the neighbor's constant badgering, shadows began to form outside the window and we heard voices. Manny and I got closer to the door like we did when mother arrived from work. We didn't hear the tugging of the knob like we'd seen Mommy do time and again. Were these the strangers Mommy had warned us about? I urgently questioned as I tugged on Manny's pajama shirt to pull him closer to me.

The voices continued. I heard a male's voice, then the neighbor's. "She leaves them home alone when she goes to work. They may be hungry. You have to do something!"

I looked at Manny. "Shhhhhh! Mommy said to be quiet. Maybe they'll go away." We huddled together and kept quiet. Suddenly a pounding on the door followed.

"Open the door!"

Frightened, we crawled to a small space behind the couch, away from the window in hopes that we wouldn't be noticed. Manny held onto me tight.

A few minutes went by and the shadows outside the window disappeared. The people seemed to have gone away. Suddenly we heard, "This is the police, open the door!" More pounding. Still, we kept quiet. "Open the door or we will break it in!"

Break the door? If they broke the door, Mommy would have to pay for it and she already worked so hard, I thought.

Finally, Manny approached the door, grabbed the knob and turned to me, terrified. Manny turned the knob and the door flew open.

His tiny body stood in front of the opened door looking up at a tall man in a uniform who asked in a deep voice, "Where are your parents?"

I ran out from behind the couch to Manny and hugged him tight. He did the same and answered in a trembling voice, "Mommy's coming home soon."

Mommy didn't come home at her usual time, so we were taken to the police station, where a lady they called "Social Worker" awaited.

In later years, I learned the agony of her decision to work overtime that day. "I was working overtime to make some extra money," she said. "I had a terrible feeling in my stomach about staying over. One hour. That's all. But I got stuck in traffic." Her eyes teared up.

That hour changed our lives forever.

I ached for my mom, already missing her. Social Worker told us she was taking us to "a new home, a new set of parents." I squeezed Manny's hand as we were led into the patrol car.

We arrived at a nice, clean and modern house somewhere in a middle-class neighborhood. Social Worker knocked on the green painted door and a blond lady opened it. "Oh you are soooo darling! And you are so handsome!" She pinched our cheeks.

Social Worker said this lady was my "New Mom" and led us outside to play.

"My New Mom?" I silently questioned. New Mom wore faded jeans and tennis shoes. Her shirt sleeves were ironed with sharp creases. She wore her blond hair at shoulder length, long enough to look cared for, yet short enough to wear it in a ponytail. I didn't want a new mom. My mother was all I needed.

Two blond-haired kids played in the yard. New Mom yelled, "Kids, come play with your new brother and sister!"

Huh? I had a new brother and sister, too? I already have Manny. Why did I need a new brother and sister? This wasn't right.

I didn't think those were her children either. Pictures of her and a man, we had yet to see were placed on top of the fireplace mantel and on the end tables. I wasn't planning on staying here very long, and it seemed neither did the other kids.

I longed for my mom. I wanted her to be with us. In retrospect, I was a strong-willed child and, having already been without my dad, my mom and Manny were all I had. Now Mom was no longer by my side. I needed the warmth of her hugs and the tenderness of her playful kisses. Manny and I stuck together, never leaving each other's side. I knew Mom would find us. Take us home. Start again.

Social Worker and New Mom led Manny and me into a room with twin beds, one on each side of the room. My bed was adorned with stuffed animals and a Barbie comforter. Pictures of fairies hung above the headboard. Manny's bed was dressed with a racing car comforter. Toy cars were arranged in a row on the dresser, ready for action. Maybe this place wasn't all that bad. We had a bed and I had Manny by my side.

"Sleep tight!" New Mom said as she tucked us both into bed.

In a quivering voice, Manny insisted, "When is my mommy picking us up?" The light from the hallway streamed into the room, onto his face. His eyes watered as he held back tears.

"We'll know more tomorrow," answered Social Worker.

The door closed behind them and New Mom's voice whispered, "I'm so glad you found us such cute kids. I hope we get to keep them." As if we were a couple of play dolls for her collection.

Manny and I lay silent in the quiet stillness of the room until the light from the hallway darkened. "Brother, brother! Mommy's coming for us," I said in a loud whisper.

"When?" He took a deep breath, then exhaled loudly.

"Soon. I know she's coming. Mommy loves us!"

Tears flowed down my face and I lay back down, attempting to fall asleep. I was emotionally drained, exhausted and concerned about Mommy. We were in this place, not home and not with Mommy.

Meanwhile, at our real home, Mommy was frantic. She later told me, "I didn't sleep that night and for many nights trying to find you. I called your tío Rey to help me, and we called the police stations, asking questions, trying to get some answers. We were given the run-around. I felt guilty and blamed myself. How could I let this happen to you?"

Feeling powerless, she cried as many tears as I did.

New Mom dressed us in new matching clothes, Manny in blue jeans and a plaid shirt and me in a jean dress with a plaid top. During meals, I was seated in a high chair and served soggy, tasteless spinach. I politely ate it. I was old enough to feed myself, but New Mom wanted to feed me.

"If your mom doesn't come for you, you'll be all mine," she said after each spoonful. "You'll be all mine."

I painfully watched Manny repeatedly resist New Mom's words and spit out the food in rebellion. I simply knew Mommy was coming for us. She wasn't going to give up. Not now. Not after she struggled to bring us to the United States for a better life. Not after she had worked hard to get us our own place to live. No doubt, leaving us home alone had not been in mother's better judgment, but she meant well. I vindicated her actions. Yet here we were. No mommy. No Papi. No tías. Alone.

Day after day for almost a month, New Mom went through her daily ritual. She was certain we would be hers. "Your mom is not coming for you. You'll be all mine by Friday."

She drove the spoon closer to my mouth and this time, restraint was not an option. I couldn't swallow my words any longer. The words were piled up inside and shot up through my throat and out my mouth with a loud thundering echo, each louder than the first, yet fading as Friday would soon be here. "My mommy loves us. She'll be here on Friday! She'll be here Friday!"

New Mom simply reached over, patted me on the head while she turned away and said, "You'll be all mine on Friday." She dismissed my words.

Friday. This was the day. Every bit of me was holding onto the memories of my mother and brother in our happy home. Her hugs. Gentle loving kisses.

The doorbell rang. New Mom answered the door. "Someone is here to visit you."

My eyes widened. I felt butterflies raging in my stomach with excitement. Could it be Mommy? I wanted so badly for Mommy to be on the other side of the door. My heart was hopeful. I walked what seemed to be miles to the open door. When Manny and I finally neared, the door opened wider.

"Mommy!" Brother yelled.

And there she was, with the strength of the sun behind her. Mommy reached down and scooped us both into her arms, hugging and kissing us. We were together again.

I didn't look back at New Mom's expression. At that point, the only thing I felt or noticed was my mom's hugs and kisses. I wished my dad would have been there, too. Instead, tío Rey was with her like he was when we were taken away.

We jumped into his car. His smiling eyes looked at me through the rearview mirror. "Let's go home," he said in a calming voice. Mom sighed loudly and turned to us with tears in her eyes, smiling.

We drove off in the car. After settling down from my excitement, I stared out the window into nothingness.

I shoved this memory far into my subconscious mind and tried to forget the fear, terror and sense of abandonment. Into the darkness the memory went, somewhere locked away, never to be remembered again. Or so I thought.

Although I drew from my inner strength and this scary time cultivated my intuition, the thought of being left alone haunted me and made my stomach clench. I became highly involved and opinionated about where we lived and many other things in life. Mom made an extra effort to reassure us everything would be okay by hugging and kissing us every moment she could.

Until I was twelve, I disengaged myself from the horrible memory of being abandoned. I finally accepted that Mom had made mistakes while she pursued her dream of a better life and followed her heart. But being a single mother of two, trying to make a living came with its challenges.

In the years that followed, mother searched for affordable housing and a steady wage.

Manny and I spent most of our grammar school years moving from city to city. Just when we'd begin to settle into school or make friends, we were off to another city. It took its toll, made me doubt my mother and long for her in other ways.

She worked relentlessly to provide for us but missed special moments like academic achievement award ceremonies. I'd scan the auditorium filled with proud parents clapping and cheering —searching—for her smiling face, yet only to be blinded with discontent. She was working and couldn't make it. Again. I still studied with the same drive mother did, making the most of *viviendo*, hoping that someday she would show up and be there for me.

Viviendo!

Mother made extra effort to ensure that someone was always watching over us. My tías visited us often in our Norwalk home. They shared my mother's tenacious energy. They all laughed and had a great time when they were together. My mother was proud to provide them a home away from home, and I looked forward to their visits. From them I learned about the true meaning of living and being the best woman I could be.

Tía Felicidad was my favorite. She saw the humor in everything and her loud laugh energized the room. She was married but traveled alone or with her children. Her visits with us were her time to get away to "Celebrate life as a free spirit," she'd say. As an entrepreneur, she bought clothing in the United States and sold it in Mexico.

My tías and family called this "*Viviendo y haciendo lo que nos gusta.*" It was living life to the fullest, with love, purpose and determination. Tía Felicidad's husband hoped she would be more of a traditional housewife, but she took *viviendo* seriously. She often said that whether right or wrong, she knew what was best for her and her family. She was carving her own path, and her family was going along for the ride. She wasn't about to allow anyone to stop her. Her beliefs and approach to life confirmed every bit of what I looked forward to in my life: to get to live the way I wanted and do what I liked. Mother shared the same philosophy, and as the eldest of her siblings, perhaps she inspired their actions.

I wanted to be like them—not a stereotypical woman—so I candidly observed and listened closely to the conversations among my aunts. I sat by their sides while they chatted about their businesses, different ways to make more money and ways to travel to visit family. The conversations were filled with carefree energy, masterminding the next move.

One day I approached Tía Felicidad and asked her to buy me a couple of bags of candy from Mexico, persuading mother to fund the purchase. Taking my mom's advice, I ordered candy that I liked, just in case the kids didn't buy them so that I would at least enjoy them myself. I requested my favorite candy *mazapán*: a peanut, crumbly dough that melted in my mouth, just heavenly. When it arrived, I excitedly emptied the first bag and counted the pieces, stacking them tall. I said, "I'll sell each piece for twenty-five cents and start early!"

I took the Mexican candy to school and sold more than a hundred pieces in two days. The kids wanted more, and so Tía Felicidad helped me import the candy from Mexico. I was making money and enjoying every minute of it until the school realized what I was doing. A letter was sent to my mom prohibiting me from continuing. The principal presented an ultimatum: stop selling or donate the money to the school. You would think I was selling drugs with that harsh ultimatum.

I was having too much fun and making too much money to stop. I found ways to work around the system by selling before and after school. Again, my business was shut down by regulating bodies, like the school board wanting a piece of the action. But I didn't stop there. This was too exciting! I was *viviendo* now, and nothing could stop me.

With the strong support of my mother and tías—and through their example—I knew that everything I explored and desired to accomplish was possible. I just had to love what I was doing and work hard to have the life that I wanted.

Home Is Where the Heart Is

For the following years until I was about sixteen, Manny and I spent our summers at Abuela Ana's house in Mexicali.

Mexicali was the place where I felt safe. It was where I felt my ancestral connection with who I am. It was my sanctuary.

When I was a little girl, I had immense energy and was happy, vivacious and full of curiosity. My golden-blonde curls bounced freely when my mother carried me in her arms. Manny and I giggled when our curiosity got the best of us as we played hide-and-seek with our cousins. The giggles echo in my memory to this day.

I enjoyed spending those days with my father. Maybe it was because of his own way of *viviendo*. Papi was a baker, and every morning at three o'clock, I'd hear the door quietly close. The sound of the muffler faded as he sped away to another day of baking bread and pastries. During his morning break, he'd pick me up and take me to the bakery, where I'd choose my favorite cream-filled glazed donut. On our way back home, he'd pop in an eight-track tape of the Beatles. We both acted out the songs as we sang; he tapped the steering wheel imitating the pulling of the guitar strings, while I held the donut close to my lips like a microphone.

Mexicali was home. Papi didn't want to move. It tore my mother up, because we felt at home there, too. I understand that now.

Papi was Abuela Ana's oldest son. Perhaps he stayed to help her. Abuela was the mother of twelve children and grandmother to more than twenty grandchildren. Still, Abuela Ana found love in her heart for another grandchild: me! Her home was the hub for generations of children. I loved to be around her. No matter the challenge, she was courageous, ambitious and had an entrepreneurial spirit. She and mom had this in common.

Abuela Ana owned her own clothing factory. Her children occasionally worked there. When I visited, I worked there to make a few pesos to spend on my adventures.

During my visits to Abuela's house, I confidently plotted my adventures and travels all over town with anticipation. I was the leader and my *primas* (cousins) happily followed along and enjoyed the adventure. I boarded the buses and used my Spanglish to ask where we were headed. My cousins laughed at my attempts and teased me about my accent. "*¡Gringa!*" they'd call me and infectiously laugh. Their teasing didn't matter, we were cousins having a good time. On these summer vacations, I learned how to drive a car, a motorcycle and, most importantly, I was free to wander about and explore. I was home.

I felt like I was becoming more and more like my mom and Abuela: taking risks, being courageous and ambitious, living a life that I was in charge of. I was happy. This was *viviendo* to me.

In Abuela's house, she provided the essentials—and plenty of love. Grandchildren fended for themselves. They cleaned the house and cooked the food. I loved being independent and creating recipes with my *primas*. The best part is that Abuela encouraged us to be independent and take the initiative. When we tried a new recipe, she'd take a taste test. "Let me see how good the food tastes. Add more salt. Spice it up a little! Make sure there's enough for your uncles."

Her stewardship helped us to shape our minds to see possibilities instead of limitations. We had to think for ourselves and listen to our hearts for answers and truths.

We usually tasted our food while we experimented, so by the time the food was ready, we were too full to have a sit-down dinner. Although the house was always filled with aunts, uncles and cousins, we rarely all sat down at once. There was a constant swinging door. The house wasn't big enough, in some ways. In other ways, Abuela Ana's cozy home had everything I needed to unleash my curiosity in the comfort of my family. I liked that I could ask questions and try to figure out solutions and if I couldn't, I'd engage my cousins restraint.

The dining room looked as though it had never been used. A chandelier hung perfectly centered over the dining table. Chairs were still wrapped in plastic and the table was dusty. Our family photo leaned on a buffet cabinet, in an 11 x 14 gold-plated frame. It was one of the last photographs we'd taken before leaving Mexicali, and there it stood timeless. I often wondered why Abuela had kept this portrait and not put it away, since my mom had left my dad. I still wanted to justify it. I was searching for my own truths.

On one occasion, I approached Abuela while she stood in front of the dusty portrait. " Abuela, why do you still have a picture of brother and me in the dining room?"

Abuela was a woman of few words. She pointed to the photo. "This is how I remember you." As she smiled, her eyes glittered.

She was five-foot-nine and towered over me. At the age of twelve, I was a mere four-foot-nine. I braced myself before I asked her the questions I'd been holding onto for years.

"Why did mommy leave Mexicali? Why didn't papi persist? Why did he give up?"

Her gentle answer was, "People make choices."

But I wanted to know more. That answer wasn't enough. "And, and, and why . . . "

She bent down, looked straight into my eyes and said, "¿Qué te dice tu corazón?" What does your heart tell you?

Well, I wasn't expecting that! I silently contemplated that question while I stared at the portrait. What did my heart say? I was happy. My mom and papi loved me. I was here with my family. The frightening days were over. I was loved!

A huge smile spread across my face. Calmness and peace softened my stern expression. The memory stayed, but I replaced the feelings I had about the babysitter, the New Mom and my mother's neglect with better thoughts of all the good things that positively affected my life. The hows and whys didn't matter. What mattered was that my heart was happy.

My high school sophomore year in 1988 marked the last summer visit to Abuela's house. The *primas* and I were learning a new meaning to boys and kissing. Abuela had her hands full and couldn't handle a house full of raging hormones. The transition from experimenting with recipes to experimenting with boys was too drastic. I was fifteen years old and Manny was seventeen. We were old enough now, by America's legal standards, to stay home alone. My tías and Abuela had planted the seed of *viviendo* and independence. I was no longer afraid. However, the instability and movement from home to home and city to city had left me feeling less grounded. I distanced myself from lasting friendships, and my interest in academics spiraled downward.

Listen to Your Heart

Manny and I hung out together. I helped him strip the paint off his prized 1968 Volkswagen bug. I started working at a fast food restaurant and became involved in the party scene. Manny discovered girls and spent time between his car and his girl, Kathy. She and I became good friends.

When my junior year in high school started, I became rebellious. With money in my pocket and new friends in the party crowd, I occasionally skipped school. I was bored.

My advanced learning went beyond the current level of teaching. I often sat in class completing future assignments while the instructor lectured. I began looking for outlets. I no longer put in the extra effort. I figured it was a matter of time before we'd move again. My disobedience led to many visits to the counselor's office. Although I was already taking college-bound courses, I wasn't being challenged enough so by the time the instructors or counselors realized I should have advanced into another course structure, I had missed too much class time and my grades had plummeted.

I also thought I knew it all, but what kid in high school doesn't? I had already started a business and I was working, making money. My mom, Abuela and tías had taught me some valuable life lessons. I wanted excitement. I found an escape with Kathy.

We got into more trouble than we could believe possible. One day, we were off to the DMV office to pay a traffic ticket she had received on one of our many excursions. Kathy was driving my brother's car, the very same one Manny had spent many hours stripping the paint off to prepare it for a new paint job. The two-seater bug had no radio, a stripped interior and required manual shifting. It might sound like a junky car, but not to my brother—and certainly not to us. We thought we were two cool chicks driving the car around town. These were our wheels.

The sun was shining brightly and both of the windows were rolled down. The warm wind blew through our hair as we conspired to contest the ticket. At five-feet tall—I sank into the battered seats—but I could still see through the bug's plentiful windshield. We traveled with traffic on a three-lane highway. The lanes were wide, with plenty of room on the road for semi-trucks and their trailers. The road was clear.

We were in the middle lane and approached a red light. Cars lined up behind us as we stopped. To our right, a semi-trailer truck carried a steel light pole twice the size of the truck. The light turned green. Kathy put the car in gear. It jolted forward. The semi-trailer truck was in front of us now. Kathy attempted to switch lanes away from the monstrous, unstable truck. The engine roared as Kathy downshifted to give the bug more torque. Our bodies jerked forward and the truck veered right.

Seemingly in slow motion, the light pole slipped off the bed of the truck and suddenly came directly toward us!

"Kathy!" I yelled out. At the same moment, a voice in my head screamed, *Move into her seat!*

I hurled myself against Kathy. I clutched the steering wheel with all my strength. My head burrowed into the side of her body. The pole came crashing into the windshield, whipping by an inch from my head, blowing past my hair like the wind had done earlier. But this was no wind! This was a twelve-foot steel pole that cut through the top of my brother's Volkswagen bug, making it an instant convertible.

The pole lifted the car and shook it like a rattle until the truck came to a stop. When the car stopped shaking, I cautiously opened my eyes, raised my head and peeked above the steering wheel. I was alive!

I should have been dead.

"Are you all right?" I asked Kathy

Dazed and shocked, she confirmed, "Yes."

A man wearing an orange hardhat was trying to pull the door open. "Unlock the door!" he yelled.

Glass was shattered all over us. Kathy carefully lifted her arm to unlock the driver side door, and we both exited.

"How did you make it out alive?" he asked.

My back was to the car. I had no idea what he was talking about. Kathy and I turned around at the same moment. The pole had ripped through the entire structure of the bug. The roof frame hung twisted into many unrecognizable shapes. The bug was actually suspended in air, held up by the pole! Light from the heavens streamed through the now mangled metal top onto the thousands of sprinkled crystals.

How had we gotten out alive? We turned to each other. Still in a daze, I hugged her. We hugged each other.

When Kathy called my brother to tell him about the accident, I heard him yell, "How's my sister? She better be okay! Why did you take her with you?"

I was reminded of that fateful day when my brother and I were kids and were taken from our mother. He had wrapped his arms around me to protect me from the pounding on the door. We had vowed to protect each other for years to come.

During the days following the accident, I pondered the divine intervention that saved my life that day, the voice that had commanded me to get into Kathy's seat. It was that same belief that reassured me when I was a little girl that my mother would return, that she would not forsake us. This time that belief was revealed as a gut instinct, an inner voice.

The more I reflected, the more I understood the power of my inner voice. Had I ignored it that day, the situation would have been deadly. After this accident, I listened carefully to my inner voice and searched for answers within my heart. I realized there was more to my core than what I really knew.

I had quelled the very person I had disciplined to study hard, earn my way to principal's honor roll and many more academic awards, time again, me—and now was the time for me to find my *viviendo*. Feel alive again.

Within a couple of days of the accident, mother went with me to the counselor's office. I demanded to go to continuation school so I could make up my credits to graduate. My file sat within arm's reach on Mr. Watt's desk, with pink slips clipped to it as evidence of disciplinary actions I was about to face resulting from the collection of truancies I had accumulated. I pressed my case until he finally gave in.

"If you go to continuation high school, you'd better promise me you'll come back your senior year," he said.

I'd need to make up thirty credits—a year's worth of course work and I had 18 months to pull it off. I promised and held out my hand to seal the deal. Mr. Watt had faith in me, yet he reluctantly shook my hand. I'm certain my mother was reciting Hail Marys in her mind while we were in the office. How the heck was I going to make this work?

A bus took students to the forsaken high school where gang members, pregnant teenagers and neglected kids went, but never really by choice. I'd heard of rare cases of people actually graduating after coming to school here. I was determined to be one of them. Students rarely showed up. At times, three students and an instructor filled the classroom. I could take as many classes as I could handle, so I home-schooled myself to speed up my learning, took night classes all year long and summer classes, too. On my high school graduation day, instead of throwing my hat and tassel in the air, I looked out into the audience in search of my mom as I had done many times before, and there she was. Mom was sitting in the stands waving furiously, letting me know she was there.

Living my life with purpose and listening to my heart was what I intended to do from this point forward. Making every moment enjoyable and doing the things I loved best.

The Heart Knows When It's Time

After high school, I graduated college with a dual business degree and I would continue my education by completing many certificate programs. From then on, I worked hard climbing the corporate ladder to leadership and management roles.

In my late twenties, I already had reached certain levels of success and my tías' message began to resonate in my mind more frequently: "*Viviendo y haciendo lo que nos gusta.*" Was I not doing what I loved?

Something was missing. I'd been in management for many years and, although it was rewarding, I was ready to reinvent myself and create new possibilities.

While I was searching the web for career postings, an "education and development" position caught my attention. The requirements listed public speaking, presentations, building teams, training and expertise in the healthcare industry. That was what I wanted to do. That was exactly the change I was looking for. The description went on to read, "Work with a fun and interactive team. Make training your career." It spoke to me. I wanted this job.

I prepared well, so it was no surprise after the interview that I was offered the position. "Congratulations, you are hired," said the director. "You'll complement the team dynamics very well."

Yes! Something new and different, challenging and exciting. I was working with a professional team of educators. We were a team of five females, including myself, varying in age and race. I was the youngest. The group reminded me of the times I'd listened to the tías mastermind about their businesses. Here, I was one of the masterminds. I wanted to believe this would be my chance to take charge of my own entrepreneurial skills—and my own destiny.

Only something wasn't right there.

To be a successful team, we had to work very well together. In the first month, each of us had taken a personality profile and we shared these with each other. My profile was the complete opposite of the others in the team. The facilitator warned us of the danger in this dynamic. I'd soon learn the realization of her words: "Joanna, you'll need to have an extra sensitivity toward your team. Your thinking will get you in trouble."

We soon experienced conflict that had to be resolved by using team-building exercises. During one session, my coworkers revealed that they felt I was very good at accomplishing goals and completing projects, but I had no sense of connection with my emotions and no expressed compassion or empathy for them. I just didn't know them.

"You're too rigid," said Felicia, a teammate. "You don't share about yourself."

How could I? Panic seized my stomach.

While Felicia went on and on, I zoned out. I was taken back to my fifth-grade year. I was ten years old. We'd moved to Merced, a town in Northern California where seasonal farmworkers lived during the crop season. The rent was cheap, the housing was decent and we were among the *campesinos*.

"El Campo" is how the kids in school referred to it, and I was tagged as one of the "El Campo" kids.

Without having or even saying much, yet dressed in our best clothes, my brother and I were labeled as *"creídos."* Arrogant. Some schoolgirls garnered attention by spreading rumors that I was going to steal boyfriends. I was only eleven, barely at the stage of puberty.

Manny and I hung out and found some solace in breakdancing and pop locking. While breakdancing had reached its pinnacle in L.A., this northern town was barely starting to see its popularity. We were invited to the local breakdancing club. Some people liked us and others didn't. It didn't matter to me. We weren't going to be there for very long and I was having fun.

When harvest season ended, the *campesinos* left town. El Campo was vacated almost overnight. Those who stayed waited out the school year.

Mother didn't wait out the school year. When news spread about our leaving town, some sixth-grade girls posted an article in the school newsletter. Leonore, the five-foot-six girl I had encouraged to stand up for herself and distance herself from the bully who verbally abused her, brought it to me. I stood in the middle of a busy playground, tetherballs swinging around me, while I looked down at the article.

"Beat It!" Signed, the 6th grade class.

Silence rippled around me. I was crushed.

Five of the sixth-grade girls gathered around me. "We didn't put that there," they said. "That's not from all the sixth graders."

The article was the talk of the school. The cowardly girls who had written the article were laughing in their circle on the other side of the playground.

My mother said not to pay them any attention. "*Son tontas,*" she'd say. They're dummies. I felt sorry for them. I looked at them, shrugged and smiled. By the end of the week, I was traveling back to L.A. I didn't let them get under my skin any more. The shield that surrounded my heart thickened.

While I listened to my teammate, Felicia, I thought, "Who are these people telling me how I should or shouldn't be? They barely know me."

Their judgment didn't sit well with me at first, yet I quickly negotiated with myself. *You want to succeed, so pay attention.* Perhaps this was part of my learning, my lesson. I finally replied, "From this point forward, I'll share more about myself. I'll start with; I've been married for nine years. I enjoy reading self-improvement books. I'm happy to be a part of this team."

We chatted about books and authors and we connected. We met regularly to organize our material. Making our training fun and using interactive learning tools added flare and excitement to the classes. The team gave each other constructive criticism to improve our classes. We were working well together. Unfortunately, this didn't last long.

To enhance my skills, I asked to take on special projects. I wanted to learn. I began leading projects. However, these projects took me away from the team. After a meeting with a manager, a misunderstanding soon shattered the team's already fragile bond.

I received an unexpected phone call. "I'm working on that project and I am the point person," Felicia declared.

I had no idea what she was talking about or what triggered her call. She was accusing me of stepping on her toes.

I kept my calm and questioned, "What project?"

Felicia raised her voice and threatened, "You better keep your hands off my project!"

When she stopped long enough to take a breath, I interjected in a serious tone, "Felicia, I'm sure this approach works for you, but it doesn't for me." *What the hell is she talking about?*

After I cooled off, I realized I had been talking with the manager Felicia worked with; perhaps she thought we had been discussing her project.

The next day, I approached her to clarify what I thought had triggered her reaction. Before I said a word, she asked, "Do you have to be involved in everything?"

"Felicia," I said calmly, "I'm not sure where you're going with this, but I assure you I will defer questions to you about this project."

She remained suspect and began to say things about me to the other team members. Now I was not only *not* sharing about myself, I was taking other teammates' projects. The team began to meet without me but still expected to collaborate. I gave the team my attention, but the attacks from Felicia came in different forms. During team meetings, she contradicted almost every word that came out of my mouth.

The first and only time a teammate came to my defense was when Monica said, "Felicia, don't you think you're over-thinking Joanna's words?"

Felicia snapped back, "Would you trust someone who tries to take your projects?"

The team fixated their eyes on me, awaiting a rebuttal.

"Felicia, don't you think it's time for us to confront this?" I asked.

"No!" She packed up her briefcase and left.

I took this hard. I had failed somewhere. How was I to work with someone who wouldn't have a conversation without animosity toward me?

After several failed attempts to talk with Felicia, I avoided her. I didn't want to be smeared and I certainly wasn't going to provide a forum for it. I became more and more involved with projects outside of the team. But hiding behind my work wasn't helping any relationship our team had at this point.

My spirit was unsettled. I needed to clear my mind. Find answers. "*¿Qué te dice tu corazón?*" My mind and heart were clouded and the answers contradicted each other. I needed to realign myself. Look deeper.

I started meditation to find my balance again. During a moment of clarity, my mother's words crossed my thoughts. "You just never stop knowing a person, you just never stop knowing." That's when it hit me. I needed to understand why Felicia was angry. I didn't really know. It was time. I called a meeting with Felicia. She pushed back hard.

"No!" she replied.

Instead, I went to her office and sat in her office chair. "Didn't I say no?" she exclaimed.

I sat there anyway. The air thickened with resistance.

"What do you want?" she questioned.

I stared her into her eyes. "I'm not going anywhere. Not from this office and not from the team."

When she said nothing, I continued. "What troubles you?"

We sat there in silence for a few moments. I wasn't leaving until I found the answer.

"You took my project," Felicia finally said. "I later found out you hadn't a clue that you'd replaced me to lead the project. I kept up the front because I was too embarrassed to apologize. I felt like a fool."

Without saying a word, I walked over to her and gave her a long hug. Not long enough for tears but long enough to show forgiveness. I didn't tell her how hard I'd taken the accusation or that it could have been disastrous to my career. Perhaps I should have approached her sooner, but my stubbornness had gotten the best of me too.

Afterward, the first couple of encounters were awkward. Felicia and I simultaneously began laughing during one of our meetings and that broke the ice. Our team noticed the difference. I began sharing a bit more about my personal life, breaking through my own cautious barrier. That barrier had stood between me and building relationships with others.

I was *viviendo* again.

I often replayed the start of the chain reaction so I would detect the signs in any future dealings. I never wanted to go through that again. One day, I sat in the employee lounge eating lunch by myself, looking out the window, reflecting. Many thoughts tumbled through my mind. And, and, and . . . .

"Joanna, it's time to move on," my heart said. "It's time." I think, in my heart, I had learned the lesson that was intended for me by working there. A bit saddened but relieved by my decision, I cleared my desk and resigned. Although the relationships would last beyond this point, there was no more energy in my heart for that place.

Love Strikes

During those tough times at work, I had leaned on my husband for his support. We'd been together for nine years and were very much in love.

When Juan and I first met, I was also cultivating another part of me. I was learning to love. Not the love that a person has for her husband, her children or even her parents, but the kind of love that balances all other emotions into one light, one whole and oneself.

I was finding my balance by learning to love myself.

By the time I was twenty, I had my own car, my own apartment, two jobs and was putting myself through college. I was happy *viviendo* and wanted more excitement in my life. My plans included traveling the world, writing novels and continuing my education. I had no desire to become a housewife like my tío wished tía Felicidad would be.

When I began dating, I thought I was simply looking for an outlet from the mundane. My life was just beginning, for goodness sakes! Marriage was a far-fetched idea. Something I knew nothing about. Yet deep down I wanted a companion, a man with compassion, smarts and someone who'd be my rock. I imagined a man who would feel my pain and give me a dose of warm words and hugs when I needed them. Someone who would care for me and make love to me without holding back. We'd travel in the dark of night to distant lands and discover uncharted treasures. Someday, the perfect man who truly loved me had to accept me for who I was and what I wanted—and accept these conditions if he wanted to join me on my life's journey.

At that time, I wanted to be single. I didn't want to commit. I wanted to keep my independence. I was enjoying my life and spoiling myself, going out with my girlfriends to clubs and meeting interesting people.

On one occasion, as we headed home from a long night of celebrating my girlfriend's birthday, we noticed a group of guys following us. They were waving and yelling out their car window. I pulled over into a parking lot to make some new friends. Little did I know, the driver, Juan, would be my future husband.

Juan and I teased and flirted with one another. We exchanged phone numbers and, to my surprise as I turned to say goodbye, he gave me a gentle kiss on my lips. Well, it was more passionate than gentle. I couldn't believe it. We had just met and he was already kissing me? He wasted no time. Although I was surprised, I must admit, I enjoyed it.

Less than a week later, Juan invited me to go to Palm Springs with him. He was moving fast. I was not.

As we continued to date, I saw many sides of him that I adored. He was kind, lovable, relentless, romantic, smart and hardworking. He was a keeper. I listened to his voice, his words and observed his demeanor. I tested his patience and questioned his intentions. He kindly persisted.

We chatted as often as time would allow, but sometimes weeks went by without seeing one another. I was focused on finishing my studies and on a mission to put myself through college. I had no time for a boyfriend. Still, he persisted in calling me every day.

During that time I worked for a restaurant chain. I traveled to increase sales at already existing restaurants and to open new ones. At one point, I was transferred but didn't let Juan know. I was entrusted to manage all of the needs of the new store: marketing, training and operations. My management position came with many challenges. My business savvy and tías' lessons contributed to my success. I was learning to love this job and I was good at it.

One night, while things were a bit quiet at the restaurant, I answered the phone and heard a familiar voice. "Were you going to call me?"

I couldn't believe he had found me! He had called all of the restaurants within a twenty-mile radius from my home. The previous restaurants were restricted from giving customers information about employees, so when he attempted to find my whereabouts, he was turned away. He relentlessly persisted. I was speechless and intrigued.

My heart was feeling something it had never felt before. At that moment, I knew this relationship was the right one for me. Although I should have—could have—questioned the effect on my *viviendo*, I didn't. "*¿Qué te dice tu corazón?*" I simply let my heart melt. Let it feel. I had found the right man and he had found me.

We began to see each other almost every day after this call. I carved out time from my busy schedule. Thoughts of the single life were overtaken by the idea of being in a committed relationship. Although I wanted to be in one, it didn't necessarily mean marriage. A lifetime commitment would be the ultimate test of knowing and trusting myself.

My mother constantly encouraged us to get married and had finally given up on the thought after she realized we were happy. I was more unsettled by the "what-ifs." What if we got tired of one another? What if he broke my heart? What if I broke his? What if we moved away again?

I had so many reservations. I didn't know what a healthy relationship was nor did I have a nuclear family to emulate. The divorce of my parents was followed by Papi's serial relationships and offspring. The quality of my mother's dating choices was effected by the marijuana- and cocaine-infused culture of the mid 1970s and throughout the eighties. Her judgment clouded by the imagery of once again finding true love. And I left with the dissolution to ever find a REAL man when I'd hear her cries from what seemed endless beatings behind the closed doors of the bedroom. The thought still makes me cringe. These conditions were enough caution to question any man's attention.

I wanted a lifetime partner.

One day my mother's loving words resonated in my mind while Juan and I were on one of our getaways. "You just never stop knowing a person, you just never stop knowing."

I was the one she'd been referring to. I would never stop knowing myself, but I didn't need to question my heart, my desires. My love for another. Now, I was ready.

Love is a time in life where the heart speaks, the mind denies and the senses desire. *¿Qué dice mi corazón?* My heart said I was in love. My heart was speaking where Juan was concerned. I wanted him in my life.

Having cultivated the intuition of the little girl who had hoped for her mother's arrival, the entrepreneur who sold candies at school, the leader who made hard choices, the survivor of a near-death experience, I was becoming the woman I would cherish. I have listened to my heart and shaped my *viviendo*, living my life the way I've want, grateful for those who fill it.

I still have a lot to learn about this woman. I may never stop knowing her completely. I will be proud and without regrets about the decisions I've made and I'll embrace what makes this journey a lifelong discovery. There is peace and beauty in the life I have chosen.

Loving my life now means asking myself, "*¿Qué te dice tu corazón?*" and I know I must listen to my inner voice and trust it. Loving my life means discovering self-love and embracing it. Loving my life means carving my path and being proud of it. Loving my life means understanding my mother's words to "never stop knowing" and accepting it. Loving my life means surrounding myself with powerful women who encourage me. After all, my heart has guided me, my tías have inspired me and my spirit has blazed new paths. Loving my life means *viviendo* and meaning it!

RITA MOSQUEDA MARMOLEJO is a public health administrator and an independent organizational development consultant, and holds a master's degree in organizational behavior. She performed her own monologue in the 2009-run of the *8 Ways to Say I Love My Life* stage production.

Running in Place

FOR MANY YEARS I HAD A RECURRING DREAM ABOUT someone or something chasing me. In my dream, I couldn't understand why I was being chased, or who it was that was chasing me. I just knew I had to get away. My only escape was to run, and I knew I had to run to save my life. I would begin running as fast and as hard as I could. As I grew tired from running, I would suddenly become aware that I wasn't getting anywhere. I wasn't moving. I was running in place, going nowhere. With the unrecognizable stalker nearing, my mind would begin racing: *I need to hide. I need to find cover. I need to be silent and still. I need to quiet my pounding heart. I need to make myself invisible and pray that the phantom pursuer doesn't find me.* Inevitably, at this point in the dream I would awaken, feeling terrified, with my heart racing, out of breath and perspiring.

Perhaps if I could have gathered the courage to turn and confront the stalker, I would have discovered much sooner that the very thing I was running from was the very same thing I was searching for. Maybe I would have come to understand a lot earlier that in order to accept myself, I had to learn to relinquish the opinions and beliefs I had unknowingly adopted. Who I was and what I wanted to become were elusive concepts that I struggled with for many years. Discovering the answer in some ways continues to be a work in progress. In other ways, it's become quite simple. But then, I'm getting ahead of the story.

Sometimes dreams are wiser than waking. —Black Elk

I grew up in Fullerton, California, at a time when Orange County was considered a bedroom community, and a drive through the county dominated by orange groves made clear the origins of its name. My first memories begin when I was four years old. I was the youngest of seven siblings. It was 1955 and the summer I learned to swim and play softball. I loved summer. Even though I was a natural at swimming and playing ball, it was through my older sister's attention that I was made to feel special.

"Ritonga," Kathryn would call out to me when she arrived home from school, "I brought you something. Pick one." She extended two curled fists that hid a piece of candy. Kathryn was nine years older, and I felt a stronger bond to her than I did to my mother.

The depth of that bond would be tested and its enduring nature would be revealed much later in life.

"Rita, is this Rita?" Kathryn whispered in an unfamiliar voice. In the darkness of night and the stillness that came with the ending of the day in our three-bedroom home, where I shared a bed with Kathryn, the rest of the family—my parents and five siblings—drifted into sleep. The voice stirred a recently stored memory created one summer night while sitting snugly among my sisters and brothers around a small fire pit—a hole dug into the ground of our bare earth-covered backyard. The fire was built with leaves, twigs and small branches from the pepper tree that canopied our lot, and small pieces of wood scavenged from our father's pile of scrap lumber reserved for house repairs. While we charred and ate marshmallows that had been held over the fire with skewers made from wire clothes hangers, Kathryn told the story about a woman who had drowned her three children. The bodies were never found. When the mother died and stood before God in judgment, her soul was condemned to endlessly walk the earth in search of her children's missing bodies. Wandering aimlessly through the night, crying, *La Llorona*, would seek out small children, sometimes mistaking an unfortunate child for one of her own. In an instant, an unlucky child could be swept away from her family and home, forever lost and eventually forgotten. Still whispering, the disguised voice called out, "Rita, this is La Llorona. I know you're not sleeping, Rita. I've come for you, Rita. Are you ready to come with me now?"

My body stiffened. I drew the blanket over my head as I dared to challenge the voice, wanting to believe it was Kathryn but uncertain who the voice belonged to or where it came from. I pleaded in my small voice, "Kathryn. Kathryn, it's you. I know it's you. Stop trying to scare me."

Fully buried under the blanket, eyes squeezed tightly shut, the voice felt detached from anything human. The slowly uttered words sounded as though they were floating through the air, reaching out for me. "This is not Kathryn. Kathryn is gone. It is I, and I am here to take you a-w-a-y."

I struggled to recognize a hint of Kathryn in this ominous sing-song voice. "Kathryn! Kathryn!" My voice rose higher, becoming louder, "KATHRYN!" I lay frozen in place, but without skipping a beat, and with all the strength I could muster, I yelled, "MAMA, MAMA, KATHRYN'S SCARING..."

Through the darkness, my father's heavily Filipino-accented voice boomed, "You keeds go to sleep."

I heard Kathryn's laughter. "Okay, go to sleep, *mocosa*, it's just me."

I breathed a sigh of relief. My sister's endearment, which meant "snot nose," assured me that it had been her all along. I felt safety and comfort in hearing the pet name she had assigned me and in the warmth of her body as she hugged me goodnight. Little did I know the reassurance I felt that night would soon dissolve into a distant memory.

In 1956 several acres of the orange grove behind our home were bulldozed and new homes were constructed. My parents bought one of the homes, and we happily relocated to our new neighborhood. Not long after settling in, my maternal grandmother passed away. Her very being had been the glue that held our family together. Within a year after grandma's passing, my parents split up and all hell broke loose.

"Start the car. Start the car. Start the fucking car!" My sister Susana and I were sitting in the Iron Dog, a beat-up 1947 Pontiac with an exposed trunk. The trunk hood had been removed because it seemed to be the best cosmetic option after a rear-end hit-and-run accident left the hood pretty banged up. Florence was sitting behind the steering wheel. We both recognized Kathryn's voice and turned to look out the rear window. We saw Kathryn and her partner-in-crime running toward the car. The two were escaping through the back entrance of a general goods store with a white man dressed in black slacks and a white shirt and tie in pursuit. My sister's arms were wrapped around a large rolled-up rug as she ran toward the car. Susana reacted immediately, starting the engine and shifting into gear, advancing the car slowly to allow the two to jump into the back seat. Before the doors were fully closed, the wheels spun into action and the burning rubber and exhaust streaming from the tail pipe created a trail of black smoke. Standing on the back seat, I stared out the rear window, stunned as I watched the man grow smaller as we sped away.

I was six years old.

In the following years, I experienced numerous police raids on our home. On one occasion, the front door was knocked off its hinges as narcotics detectives and police officers stormed into our home searching for Kathryn and her cache of heroin. There never really was a cache to be found, however, because her habit was far greater than her ability to maintain a supply large enough to market.

I can't say that I know when or how drugs slithered into our home. I only know for sure the cancerous effect it had on our family.

I witnessed a few of Kathryn's friends overdosing from heroin in our home, and their subsequent recovery after being drenched, fully clothed, in a cold shower, forced to stand and walk while braced between two individuals who literally dragged the nearly comatose person back into consciousness. Once the person regained sufficient awareness, she was forced-fed large quantities of cold milk and hot coffee. Within a few hours, she walked out of the house fully revived and unaccompanied, as though there had never been a near-brush with death.

Addiction consumes: first the self and then the others within its orbit. —Gabor Mate, M.D.

During one of the raids on our home, my two brothers and I were taken to the police station along with Kathryn, who was babysitting us. At sixteen years old, she was strung out on heroin and was eight months pregnant. It wasn't until the following morning that my mother discovered the note from the police, explaining that her children could be reclaimed from the police station. When she didn't appear for us that first evening, my brothers and I were taken to the Crittenton Orphanage, where we would live for several weeks. Kathryn was delivered to juvenile hall where she would give birth to my nephew. My mother eventually convinced the court that she could provide supervision and a safe home for her children.

Just days after my brothers and I returned home from the orphanage, Becky, Ana and Sandra, my neighborhood playmates, were outdoors playing with their dolls. I joined them and was received by Ana's warning: "My parents don't want me to play with you anymore because they say your sisters are bad and you're going to grow up to be like them."

On that day, in my eighth year of life, it felt as if a message had been engraved on my forehead: *Rita is no good*. Those words wormed their way into my heart and ate away at my self-esteem as I grew up.

I remember the first time I was asked, "What do you want to do when you grow up?"

I was ten years old.

Mr. Allen was the principal at the elementary school I attended. I was called to his office the morning following an annual open house event and my debut performance in a duet with one of my fifth-grade classmates. "Rita, I want you to know we're very proud of you. You did a fine job last night. Have you thought about what you want to do when you grow up?"

I didn't skip a beat. "Yes. I want to be an opera singer."

His eyes widened and he opened his mouth but no sound came out. He quickly regained his composure and made a few more statements I didn't pay attention to because I became engrossed in my own thoughts. Why had he reacted that way? And where had the idea of me becoming an opera singer come from to begin with? The only opera singer I had ever seen was on a black and white television in a slap-stick comedy show featuring the Marx Brothers, yet I had spoken the first thing that had come to mind.

Perhaps he had not expected any answer, because there seemed to be a common, unspoken understanding among most of the adults in my world: I would become a drug addict and prostitute. How could I not?

I remember one such adult. "What's your name?" asked the Catholic worker whose charitable work at the church included distributing gowns to the young candidates preparing for their Confirmation. The Confirmation ceremony is one of seven sacraments in the Catholic religion, and it marks the passage into adulthood while further binding the candidate to the Church. I was proudly counted among the candidates. The church volunteer distributing the gowns was a short, dark-skinned, rotund and stoic-looking woman. Her jet black hair pulled back into a bun accentuated her round face and wide, jutting mouth. I recognized the woman from my neighborhood, although I didn't know her personally. I didn't imagine she would know who I was, after all, I was just a kid. But apparently she did know, because upon hearing my name, she handed me my gown as though she feared contracting a communicable disease. Her words spewed out in disdain. "Oh, you're one of *them*." The sting of her rebuke felt like a sharp slap to my face. I had heard similar accusations before, but I never imagined I would be subjected to such hatred in church.

I was with several of my friends who were waiting with others for their gowns in the room with us that day. All I could hear was the giggling that came from behind me. I turned to look at my friends and thought I saw bemusement in their faces. I felt humiliated. I wanted to run and hide, but instead I stood quietly and said nothing. On the walk home, the anger began rising and I could no longer contain my feelings.

"Who does that fat ugly frog-face think she is?" I ranted. "What did I do to her? She's supposed to be with the church. She's not supposed to say shit like that! I hope she burns in hell."

I don't recall anyone saying much of anything for the rest of the walk home. As angry as I felt toward the woman, I felt equally hurt by my friends' reactions, or non-reactions. How could they laugh? How could they not defend me?

Nothing was ever again mentioned about the incident, not by me nor any of my friends. However, the message I received that day as I prepared to dedicate myself to God and the Catholic Church was that no matter what I did or did not do, I would never be accepted on my own merit.

There was one adult, however, who loomed larger than life in my world. I was in the fifth grade when I met Sara, my best friend's mother. Sylvia and I had met at the beginning of the school year and we quickly discovered our lives were in stark contrast to one another. Sylvia's home was always clean, there was always food in the refrigerator and pantry, the family sat at the table together for meals, the adults—Sylvia's parents, Sara and Paco—ran their household lovingly and with an iron fist, and many of Sylvia's extended family lived within three blocks of one another. In my home, on the other hand, the few extended family members we were familiar with may have lived close in proximity but were extremely remote in terms of involvement. My dad's gambling sometimes took priority over the needs of his family. There were occasions—fortunately not often—when my brothers and I went to bed with pangs of hunger because there was no food in the house. My mother nearly always was at home when I returned from school and she always appeared to be attending to one thing or other around the house, yet there was often disorder and chaos. My mother seemed child-like to me, with limited ability for coping with the demands that life presented. My siblings and I had no restrictions placed on us, and we had free reign to come and go as we pleased.

"I hate my life!" Sylvia complained one day on our walk home from school. "I wish I could be like you. You can do whatever you want."

"Don't say that," I admonished her. "You don't know what you're saying. I wish I had someone to tell me what to do."

At ten years old, I understood that I was on my own, and I was able to recognize what was missing. Being self-reliant and independent had its advantages, but I would have willingly traded my freedom for adult guidance.

I was grateful for Sara's no-nonsense approach. Early in our relationship, Sara made it very clear that I would always be welcomed, as long as I remained respectful and trustworthy when I entered through the doors of her home. I carefully walked the straight and narrow when it came to Sara, and I was rewarded with Sara inviting me into her life and creating a place of respite for me within her home and family. Sara served as sponsor for my Confirmation and she officially became my godmother. Sara gave me hope for the future, but I still felt alone.

When I was fourteen, I began dating my first boyfriend, Diego, who was sixteen years old. Diego was Sara's older brother, and I'd had a crush on him from the moment I first saw him, when I was ten years old. At fifteen, he had dropped out of high school and began working in a factory. He was incredibly handsome, funny, popular, always had money in his pocket and was the owner of a shiny, lowered 1959 blue Chevy Impala that had chrome tail pipes, loud mufflers and a chrome record player bolted to the bottom of the car dashboard that played his prized collection of 45 rpm's. Sitting next to Diego, as we cruised through town, felt like I was riding in the town parade.

Because I was starved for affection, Diego's interest in me boosted my sense of worth. I not only held his attention, but I was also the envy of many young women who would have loved to trade places with me. I was living a dream.

My resolve to remain a virgin melted with Diego's persistence and the intoxicating delirium born from the sensation of feeling loved and wanted. In the beginning of our intensely passionate relationship, I began imagining a future, a concept I had only once briefly visited when four years earlier my school principal had inquired about my career goal.

Diego and I planned to get pregnant. We concluded the only way we would receive permission from our parents to marry would be if we were pregnant. Frankly, it was more about getting permission from his parents, since I had been making my own decisions for a long time. We thought we had it all worked out, but we failed to consider what might be needed after the marriage. After all, didn't people in love live happily ever after? We were kids and all we knew was that we wanted to be together. There were a few other serious problems, though, like Diego's insecurity and violence, and my cutting wit and temper—an explosive combination.

Diego was extremely jealous, and like Dr. Jekyll and Mr. Hyde, on a turn of a dime he could fly into a rage and become verbally and physically abusive. At first I interpreted his possessiveness as love. I felt proud that someone could care so much for me. But what first felt flattering soon became frightening and abusive. The abuse slowly began after we became physically intimate. It started with verbal lashings. "Why are you looking at him?" he would ask as we passed a stranger. If I had the misfortune of turning my head in the direction where anyone of the opposite sex, regardless of age, might coincidentally be within range of sight, Diego's tongue lashing would begin: "You want to screw him, don't you, you fucking whore." In his mind, the slightest gesture of sociability or curiosity in anything or anyone was evidence that I was on the prowl behind his back.

The first time Diego struck me came without warning. We had pulled into the neighborhood gas station for a fill-up. In 1966, gas stations were still service stations where the attendant pumped the gas, checked the fluids under the hood and washed the windshield. On this day, the attendant—a clean-cut married man in his early twenties who we both casually knew from the neighborhood—smiled at me as he cleaned and polished the windshield. I had no idea the attendant's innocent gesture had caused Diego's temper to flare, until we drove away. As he maneuvered the car onto the road, his fist went sailing through the air, landing hard against my head. He said I had disrespected him by returning the attendant's smile.

When his anger subsided, he was remorseful. He promised it would never happen again. It did, many times after that.

As his verbal abuse became more belittling and the physical abuse became more violent, I learned that it was much safer to behave aloof and disinterested in anyone or anything for fear that even the slightest sign of curiosity could trigger a berating and beating.

I tried breaking off the relationship, but we were in too deep. I wanted to believe his promises of change; and I believed his insistence that no other man would ever be interested in me because I was no longer a virgin. I felt trapped. I couldn't reach out to anyone. I couldn't tell anyone what was going on because I reasoned I would have to reveal that I was no longer a virgin. I was too ashamed to make such a confession. Instead of breaking off the relationship, I began changing my behavior to appease him. I stopped cracking jokes or remarking on whatever came to mind. I began withdrawing, keeping my thoughts to myself out of fear that something innocently spoken could ignite his short fuse.

By 1967 the Vietnam War was raging and many of the young men in our barrio were drafted into the Army while a few, including my two brothers, Eddie and Michael, enlisted in the Marine Corps. Diego and my brothers were good friends. My brothers' enlistment—along with seeing other guys in the barrio return on leave from boot camp looking, walking and talking differently—motivated Diego to follow suit. He, too, enlisted in the Marine Corps.

By the time he left for boot camp, I was pregnant. The only way I could think to camouflage and delay dealing with the dramatic changes that were occurring in my body and in my life was to suck in my gut and wear loose fitting clothes. As my ninety-six pound frame began filling out, my gangly, rectangular five-foot two-inch girlish body looked like it was blossoming with a softening of angles, developing into a woman's shape. As my belly grew, my posture began subtly changing to adapt to the camouflage I was attempting to create and causing my derriere to protrude. By this time, I had isolated myself from family and friends.

I was fifteen years old.

Diego was too jealous for me to maintain any friendships. And both of my brothers were in Vietnam, my father had begun a new family, my sisters were involved in their lives and my mother lived in her own little private world. While Diego was away at boot camp, I had to carefully walk a tightrope. My socializing was restricted to his family. I was aware that news traveled fast in the barrio, and that any behavior on my part that could be misconstrued as an indiscretion by his friends or relatives would quickly find its way to Diego. I feared the wrath that would strike if such a nightmarish situation materialized.

There was something even more menacing that worked at keeping me isolated and prevented me from reaching out for help: I had become my own worst enemy. I came to believe the abuse was my fault. If only I were prettier, shapelier, had a better family, was more interesting. . . . No. I had to hide the truth because the truth translated into *Rita is no good*. I decided I would prove to the world that I was good and decent: I would be honorable and dutifully wait for my man to return home. I was certain my worthiness would come to be recognized. My strategy soon began working. I began receiving accolades from his family for my loyalty.

When Diego was home on leave, we were married in civil court. "How do you feel," my father-in-law asked the moment we entered his house.

In unison we both responded, "No different." We were overwhelmed with the circumstances of our lives, making every effort to behave like adults. Diego was scheduled to ship out to Vietnam in two months and he was terrified about the idea. The war was no longer a vague concept, and the gravity of his decision to become a marine became pressingly real for him. Reality in my life boiled down to being vigilant about not riling Diego's insecurities.

My father-in-law remarked, "Ah, you guys aren't in love!" Maybe he was right. Maybe we weren't in love; maybe we were just in need of one another. Maybe needing someone that you can unleash your pain and frustration or project your own insecurities onto is more compelling and, in a twisted way, is at least equally as strong as love.

When my contractions began in the early evening of December 12, 1967, I concluded the dinner I had that night was responsible for the discomfort I was feeling. It was only after everyone had retired for the night that I realized the intermittent pains I was experiencing were due to the start of labor. It was a weekday and Diego was living on base in San Clemente. Paco, Sara and my mother accompanied me to the County General Hospital where I was ushered to an examination room. As soon as the nurse completed the examination, she quickly removed her gloves, telephoned the doctor, and reported, "Well, she must be very brave because she's dilated four centimeters and she isn't showing any signs of discomfort." I had no idea what four centimeters meant but based on the one-sided conversation I had been privy to, I figured I would be giving birth at any moment and I also felt very confident that the birthing process was going to be a walk in the park. It didn't take long to learn differently.

By midnight, I was writhing in pain, heavily sedated, and left alone in a closet-sized labor room that accommodated little more than a hospital bed. In 1967, no one, other than medical personnel, was allowed to be with the mother during labor or delivery. A nurse would come into the room to check on me periodically, but my progress was managed primarily via a metal speaker box attached to the wall that was positioned within arm's reach so that I could press a button to communicate with the nurse posted at the nursing station. My memory of labor is sketchy, but I do recall repeatedly calling for help to go to the bathroom. I was informed it was the baby's head pushing down and that the pressure created the same feeling, and I did not need to go to the bathroom. Approximately thirty-two hours after arriving at the hospital, my infant was born, and it was a few hours later that I recall Diego waking me and proudly announcing that we had a boy.

In keeping with routine medical practice for uncomplicated deliveries, my infant son and I were discharged from the hospital when he was three days old. I was mesmerized by my infant and in disbelief that I had a role in bringing anything so beautiful into the world. A day or so after returning home from the hospital, I was innocently and curiously asked by my friend, Sylvia, who was now also my sister-in-law, "where does the baby come out from?" Although I had given birth and was recovering from the stitches that served to repair the body's natural response to delivering a 7 pound 14 ounce infant, I simply couldn't envision any other answer, and replied, "From the butt."

I was sixteen years old.

As a teenage mother living at my in-laws' home—a battered bride to a soldier in combat who was capable of controlling my behavior from thousands of miles away—I found respite in the neighborhood Spanish-speaking Baptist church. It was in the safety of the outstretched arms, the uplifting songs and testimonies, and the approving smiles that I found relief from the despair and hopelessness that defined my existence. I accepted as truth the belief that if I was a faithful servant to God, my prayers would be answered. Yet, I was so disconnected from my emotions, so intent in my belief that my life began and ended with my abusive husband, that I wasn't even capable of praying for change in my own life. Instead, I prayed for my sister, Kathryn, to find redemption.

I trusted that somewhere, something, someone—that this omnipotent Being above—would miraculously reach down into my world, into my life, and like a genie in a bottle, grant me my wish. Wishing for a rescue for me was unfathomable, so I wished for the next best thing: for my sister, Kathryn, to pull her life together. Maybe I unconsciously imagined my sister rescuing me, if only she could just straighten out her own life.

In July of 1968 Diego was wounded in action. He was transferred to Japan to recuperate from shrapnel wounds. Two years after joining the military, Diego was decorated with a purple heart and honorably discharged. However, the psychological trauma he suffered in heavy combat on the front lines was never diagnosed. Diego's psyche, which had been fragile before he entered the military, became even more fragile from his experience in Vietnam. Within two months after his discharge, Diego developed a full-blown habit and was strung out on heroin.

I was pregnant with our second son.

Diego's addiction had spiraled out of control by the time our second child was born and he was committing robberies or stealing merchandise from department stores and then selling the stolen goods to purchase his drugs. His illegal activities led to repeated arrests. Torn between upholding my vows of marriage and the desire to provide my babies with a stable home environment, I sought advice from the one objective voice of authority I knew: my obstetrician.

At my post-delivery examination, I began "Dr. Peterson, what is the chance of a heroin addict stopping using heroin?" I felt ashamed my husband was a heroin addict and was uncomfortable speaking so honestly or privately with anyone, but I knew I needed help with making a decision.

He paused before answering, and then simply said, "It's not impossible, but it's highly unlikely. It's a very difficult drug to overcome, and most people who become addicted will never break the habit. They usually end up dead from an overdose or in prison."

I would spend another two years in conflict about whether to leave or stay in the marriage, but once I made the decision to leave, I knew there would be no turning back. During one of Diego's incarcerations, my boys and I moved out of my in-laws' home and in with my sister, Susana. I would eventually file for divorce.

I was twenty years old.

I was still leap-years away from understanding how my choices had a direct effect on what my life looked like. I did know I wanted a better life for myself and my boys. I enrolled in a War on Poverty secretarial training program, and in less than two months I had sharpened the business and typing skills I had learned in my ninth grade business skills class. I earned a general equivalency diploma and became employed as a clerk typist at an engineering firm. Our world and our lives were changing, yet I continued to carry the deeply rooted belief that I was no good.

We had been living at my sister Susana's for about two weeks when out of the blue Kathryn appeared. "Rita, will you give me a ride," Kathryn asked almost immediately upon entering Susana's home. "I owe this dude a favor and I need to score some *carga* for him. He'll wait here until we get back with the *dope*."

I had not seen Kathryn in months. Her return from what I believed was a nearly one-year hitchhiking escapade through the United States and Canada was unexpected. (I later learned she had just finished serving a one-year prison sentence for a drug-related crime.) It was the first in a very long time since I had seen her looking so healthy. In the year that Kathryn had been gone, she clearly had stopped using drugs. Her body was fit and filled out, her hair was long, thick and shiny, and her fair skin was suntanned gold. She looked beautiful, and her very presence brightened the room and filled my heart with hope. The child in me kicked in and once again I became the little sister.

"Are you sure it's not for you, Kathryn?" I asked.

As I stood staring into her eyes, searching for the truth, the image that ran through my mind was the last time I had seen her. She had been strung out and had come looking for me at my in-laws. Diego had not been home at the time, but the mere mention that my sister had been there would have been enough to ignite his fuse and send him into a rage. In an effort to avert the potential abuse, I did not invite her in. Before my sister could even offer a greeting, I anticipated what she wanted, rudely told her I had no money and explained I was busy. I still felt guilty for the way I had behaved toward her and I wanted to make it right.

The fear of Diego's disapproval no longer loomed over me, and I wanted to help her out, but I didn't want to be a part of any drug deals. As much as I wanted to say no, I couldn't. I rationalized to myself that she needed to know how much I cared about her and that I would help her out with whatever she needed. The real truth, though, was that I feared Kathryn's rejection.

"Are you sure you're not going to get high?" I wanted to believe her and ignore the feeling I had that whatever she said would be a lie. Agreeing to drive her felt wrong, but the thought of saying no was terrifying. Paying attention to my feelings was not as important as having assurance of Kathryn's love and approval. I needed to regain that sense of safety and security I had once known with her.

"No," she assured me, "I just need to get rid of this dude but I owe him this favor."

I made my decision in a blink of the eye, but it felt like a lifetime had passed before I finally arrived at the answer. "Okay."

Kathryn was opening the car door before I had the gear shifted into park as we pulled in front of the connection's two-story home. "I'll be right out," she announced, instructing me to wait in the car.

I sat there for at least twenty minutes, listening to the radio and enjoying the unplanned time alone, when the front door opened. Instead of Kathryn, her connection emerged, walking briskly toward me. The car window was rolled down and he bent at the waist, lowering himself to meet me at eye level, yet avoiding looking into my eyes. He crossed his arms, resting them on the window sill, gripping something in his right hand as his eyes furtively scanned the neighborhood. In a low but urgent voice, he said, "Take this to the dude that's at the house." He unclenched his fist, releasing into my hand a balloon the size of a small apricot. "Kathryn overdosed. My old lady has her in the shower right now. As soon as I go back in, we'll start walking her around and we'll feed her some coffee. Don't worry. We'll take care of her. Just take this to that dude and tell him Kathryn said she decided to stay here and she'll catch up with him later."

I knew there was no time for questioning. The next few minutes were crucial. Time could not be wasted. I trusted he would take care of her. I drove home as instructed, delivered the balloon and message, and her friend left. I had become an accomplice in this illegal drug deal and I just wanted to get through the night and wipe it out of my memory as quickly as possible, promising myself that I would never again do anything so stupid.

At least an hour later the telephone rang. I absentmindedly answered, distraught and lost in the despair I felt with the knowledge that Kathryn's using had resumed. "Hello."

It was Kathryn's drug dealer. "Rita, I can't bring her out. We've done everything and she won't come to. She needs to go to the hospital. I'm going to bring her to you. You'll have to take her."

The words suddenly registered, shocking me into the present.

"No, don't bring her to me, take her to the hospital."

He was not willing to implicate himself by delivering a drug-overdosed addict to the hospital, so he brought her to us. I was outside waiting when they arrived. I moved quickly, running around to the driver's side of the car to get to Kathryn. I wrapped my arms around her and with her back against my chest I pulled her out of the car.

"Huhhhhhhhhh." That was the last sound I ever heard from my sister, Kathryn, as I felt the air emptying out of her lungs and life escaping her body. A few hours later Kathryn was pronounced dead at the hospital.

I have very little memory of the days that followed or of the funeral. I am so grateful that my oldest sister, Connie, had the presence of mind to see through her own grief to recognize that I was teetering toward a nervous breakdown. I do remember as Connie was preparing to return to her home in New York, that she asked me, "Rita, why don't you and the boys come to New York with me? Take a break. You can come back whenever you're ready."

The next day we were on a flight to John F. Kennedy Airport. Before leaving, I telephoned my manager, who arranged my leave of absence and suggested that I contact one of our division's computer suppliers if I decided to work while I was in New York. Within four days of arriving in the Big Apple, I was working in Manhattan. From the moment that I arrived, my mind was occupied with getting to know our new surroundings and learning my way around the city. My oldest child was in kindergarten, and I enrolled him in school. The circumstances demanded my attention, and at the end of each day I was too tired to think or feel. The few months that we spent in New York were just enough time and distance from my broken marriage and Kathryn's death to prepare me for the next blow that was to come.

We were summoned back to California one Sunday afternoon by my father-in-law. "Rita, Sara's cancer is eating her up. She has big sores all over her body." Sara had been diagnosed with cancer several weeks before Kathryn's death, but she had lived and worked with debilitating pain for several years before finally receiving a diagnosis of breast cancer. Sara was a modest Mexican-American woman and did not like the idea of exposing her body to mere strangers, regardless of their professional status. By the time Sara conceded to visiting a doctor, the cancer had spread to her major organs and bone marrow, causing a deterioration in her hip bone that rendered her immobile and caused her excruciating pain. Paco continued, "She says the only ones she will let take care of her are you and me. Rita, I don't know what to do. Can you come home?"

We returned home that evening. We were simple, uneducated people, and when Sara learned she had only a few months to live, she chose to live those months out at home, with absolutely no medication to soften the ravaging of her body.

Four months after Kathryn's death, Sara passed away, following a long and painful battle with breast cancer. Any thoughts I may have entertained of ever living a happy and satisfying life were buried with Kathryn and Sara, along with my belief that the Church and God would remedy my troubles. I had believed God would save my sister Kathryn, and instead both she and Sara were dead. Once again, I was all alone, only this time, I decided, the only person I could depend on was myself. As far as I was concerned, God did not exist.

I began pursuing activities that could distract me from the chaotic and incessant gnawing on my heart, soul and mind. I was always in motion, it seemed, constantly running from one thing to another, focusing my attention and energy on a job, my boys' after-school activities, an academic pursuit, a cause or injustice, and on a couple of occasions, a romantic relationship. The more unbearable the pain of loss and loneliness became, the more I wrapped my life around distractions. I surrendered my attention to anything that could keep my mind active, diverting me from the pain and emptiness I felt.

It was 1979 and as a struggling single parent, I was fortunate to have secured a sales position with the printing division of a Fortune 500 company.

I was twenty-eight years old.

My peers at work were college graduates, but as a high school dropout, I could neither recognize nor appreciate my own accomplishments. Instead, I only focused on what I lacked.

There was no question that I had become an exception to the rule. I wasn't a prostitute or drug addict, but I still felt alone. At every turn, I felt like the outsider, a misfit. I had begun to build a foundation that supported my family's material needs, even offering us some luxuries to enjoy and new possibilities in life to explore. However, the emptiness and loneliness I felt were unbearable and never went away.

Distraction served as my pain medication, but the effect also nullified any sense of accomplishment or joy I might otherwise have known. Although my future in the printing business promised increased success and a comfortable lifestyle, I began to believe that the answer to my dilemma could be found through education. Formal education would serve as the be-all, end-all solution to my feelings of emptiness, uprootedness and alienation. I imagined that through education, I could create a circle of relationships where I would finally fit in. If I had a formal education, then I would become someone of value.

Everything in my life felt overwhelming and unmanageable: the isolation and emptiness, the image I felt compelled to present as a cheerful, fun-loving, free-spirited, ambitious and liberated woman, the demands and challenges of single parenting. I had many roles and I didn't know how to integrate them. I often felt I was living separate lives. I felt like a deflated ball in the middle of the ocean, barely staying afloat, being tossed about in unfriendly, choppy waters. I needed to feel anchored, secure and whole. I needed a lifeline. I needed to make a change.

I was thirty-one years old.

I resigned from my job as account executive with the Fortune 500 company to become a full-time student. Although I had discussed the change with my children and we all were on board about the dramatic changes we thought we knew we would have to make, living with the reality of surviving on the meager income I earned from a part-time job and the small government loan I received was much different from the romanticized idea I had imagined. I began escaping our dismal reality by smoking marijuana and having a relationship with a man who was everything I wanted to be. He was brilliant, educated, kind, generous, Chicano and an investigative reporter for a major media network.

Marcos had no interest in parenting two pre-adolescent boys. Still, I continued to date him, hooked on what he offered because I believed it was the closest I could ever possibly get to realizing the dream I flirted with: becoming a writer. I admired Marcos. He was kind and gentle, and I grew to love him. The activities, the events, the places and people I was exposed to through Marcos created a fantasy world for me, allowing me to experience life through the achievements of another. Although I secretly wanted to become a journalist, dreaming was a luxury I no longer dared entertain. Avoiding dreaming was one way of minimizing disappointment. And Marcos's habit of constantly correcting my speech and grammar reinforced my idea that I simply wasn't good enough to become a writer.

It wasn't long before my boys began experimenting with drugs. They quickly graduated to smoking PCP, a synthetic illegal drug. Encounters with the law led to being locked up in juvenile hall. The message I communicated loudly stated that I preferred Marcos over my boys. I never intended to make such a statement, but similar to the drug addict—crazed and driven by the need for the next fix—I was similarly addicted to the distraction that kept me a safe distance from my pain. The family legacy stretched far and deep, and breaking the cycle would not come easily.

The day I met Julio in the school cafeteria marks the day I would begin to discover tools that would help me learn to quiet my mind in order to look inward. It was the beginning of the school year, 1988, and we were both working on new assignments as teachers for the Los Angeles Unified School District. I had just completed a bachelor's degree and was hired with an emergency teaching credential. During lunch break, we sat together in the cafeteria. When he asked if I knew who my ancestors were, I thought he was asking if I had traced my genealogical history.

I replied, "I'm definitely interested in finding out who my ancestors are, but I just haven't done the research yet."

"I can help you find who your relatives are. I have a teacher that I work with. If you're interested, I can introduce you to him," Julio offered.

I was thrilled with the offer.

I grew up without an extended family, and discovering my family lineage had been a long-burning desire.

"I would love to meet him." I finally had the time and energy, and I certainly had the desire to dedicate myself to doing the necessary research.

The research ended up being nothing like what I imagined.

Several months after the conversation with Julio, I was experiencing my first sweat lodge ceremony that was facilitated by Lone Walker, a Korean War veteran from the Dakota Nation. Lone Walker was the friend Julio had spoken of, and Julio's offer to help me find my relatives was another way of saying, "I can help you find spiritual healing."

I was thirty-eight years old.

Through ceremony, while sharing in songs and prayers, I began learning how to sit with myself, to practice daily prayer and to examine my thoughts in order to reprogram them. These were exactly the medicine and tools I needed to begin building a sense of wholeness. Through ceremony I also began building a network of friends and associates.

Innocently accepting Julio's invitation on that day in the cafeteria was a pivotal point in my life. My introduction to Native American tradition was one more step in my journey toward reconciling my past and learning to live in the present. The spiritual muscle gained from practicing traditional ceremony was key in helping me reconnect with my humanity. It was only after repeatedly submitting to intense, physically demanding conditions that I eventually learned to surrender my will and not resist the elements, but rather to sit with them. It was through traditional training that I began learning to quiet my mind long enough to distance myself from the long-held negative ideas that had taken root in my head—but there were many.

I believed I was ugly, stupid and ruined. As a child, I was an outcast in my own community. My future was predicted by the authority figures and adults in my world: I would become a drug addict and prostitute. I had never seen myself as worthy—until now. From within the darkness, I could discern a bit of light.

I still needed to learn to accept and love myself, but how could I learn to love myself when I resisted confronting many demons that remained lurking in the dark recesses of my mind. One of the most self-destructive demons that I battled with for nearly half a century was rage. Although the slightest inconvenience or annoyance could result in me losing my temper, there was one person in particular who served as a trigger for my anger. That person was my mother, and I often could not spend more than twenty minutes with her without becoming enraged. Up until the last year of her life, I had a love-hate relationship with her.

I loved her. She was sweet, gentle, kind. And I hated her. I experienced her as incompetent and incapable of hearing or understanding anything I may have wanted to communicate to her. She had a total loss of hearing in one ear and diminished hearing in the other, and her ability to comprehend ideas and concepts was equally limited. I felt guilty that I didn't have more compassion for her, and then I would feel angry for feeling guilty. I was stuck in this conundrum of love-hate emotions toward her.

In Lak 'ech: I am your other you. —A Mayan phrase

According to my father, my mother "went crazy" after I was born. In 1951, immediately after giving birth to me, she was given a hysterectomy. It seems the hormonal imbalance that was caused by the hysterectomy is what led to my father labeling my mother as "crazy." I don't know what it was exactly that caused my mother's mental health to deteriorate. Whether it was a direct result of the hysterectomy or if there was a predisposition that was triggered by the hysterectomy, I just know that the mother I grew up with had very limited coping skills.

It wasn't until she was in her seventies, when she was hospitalized for a stroke, that I learned that her limitations were related to mental illness. While visiting my mother one day during her hospitalization, I opened her medical chart, which had been left at the foot of her bed.

My mother had been diagnosed as paranoid-schizoid.

As the youngest of seven siblings, as a child, I became the parent in my relationship with my mother. It often felt as though I was the one who had to make decisions for her. I needed to look after her, and I resented it. Throughout my adulthood, I stubbornly resisted accepting my mother for who she was. I persisted in wanting a different relationship with her, the one I had wished for as a child.

Take the week before the Christmas of 2000, my mother's last Christmas with us. I began imagining a kitchen filled with laughter and chatter. In my mind, I could smell the fresh pine aroma from the Christmas tree. I could see the multi-colored lights blinking off and on, and I could feel the anticipation and pride of tasting the first batch of tamales made with the help of my youngest child—who was eight years old—my grandson and my mother. I had started the tradition of making tamales during the winter holidays several years earlier. And although I hadn't quite perfected the recipe, the whole family activity idea seemed like a great plan, so I prepared the ingredients and then drove to Orange County to bring my mother over to help with the tamales and memory-making intimate family event.

I had an active imagination.

I certainly could have predicted the outcome, if I hadn't been so driven to create the fantasy of a nurturing mother-daughter relationship with the sage grandmother who shared stories with her grandchildren as we all happily made tamales together. Instead, within ten minutes, I became exasperated, feeling as though I was instructing three children, each with ten thumbs, in the art of making tamales. Once again I was forced into the role of having to parent my mother. I soon became angry and verbally abusive toward her. Just as always, after my emotional and verbal eruptions, I felt miserable for behaving the way I did, angry because I could never get what I wanted, and resentful that life was so unfair.

There I was in the kitchen, once again all alone after pushing everyone away with my criticism and anger. I was deep in thought, feeling guilty and confused, when I suddenly realized how crazy my behavior was.

I heard myself silently asking, *Why do you keep doing the same thing over and over, trying to get a different result, when there's no reason to believe anything will be different? Who's crazy here?*

After more than forty years of foiled attempts to create something I fantasized about in a mother-daughter relationship, I was able to recognize that it would be impossible to ever satisfy that child's yearning for bonding with her at the level I ached for. I had to let go. My mother would never be able to fill that role for me. In that moment, I realized: Rita, it's time to take care of yourself.

I was finally able to accept my mother and to let go of the anger and resentment I had unconsciously harbored for all those years. Feelings of forgiveness slowly began replacing the anger, and I began experiencing moments of peace and a sense of completeness. Self-acceptance was born from that moment of awareness, along with the understanding of self-responsibility and self-care.

I was forty-nine years old.

These were hard-learned lessons that came late in life. I am still learning. Being able to say, "I love my life," means being able to genuinely say, "I love myself." For decades, I believed that loving my life meant that I had to have a dream job that generated a dream income so that I could live a dream life with a dream mate in a dream home with a dream family. But I was always running after the dream and running away from myself.

I believe that by practicing age-old traditions and teachings, my mind, heart and spirit began to heal. I believe the mental and spiritual discipline I developed through ceremony eventually enabled me to disengage from the cycle of self-delusion I'd been stuck in for all those years. Little by little, one step at a time, I have learned to celebrate the beauty in life and to accept with gratitude that each day brings the opportunity to create anew and to strengthen bonds.

Although I was blindsided and deeply wounded by Kathryn's and Sara's deaths, the one truth I gained from their passing is that life is cyclical, like the seasons. I believe it was through their deaths that my life was resurrected. When Kathryn and Sara died, I was left with a huge gaping wound. I rejected the idea of God, and there was nothing left to replace the hollowness. The pain and emptiness I felt was excruciating. At first, my attempts to escape the pain and fill the void propelled me into constant motion. I was perpetually on the move, searching for distractions and focusing my attention on whatever could hold my interest. Through the distractions, I found temporary relief from the anxiety that was always bubbling inside me—just below the surface of awareness—like a volcano silently preparing to erupt. As hard as I may have tried during my waking moments to avoid looking at myself, during sleep and through my recurring dream of running in place, something was nudging me, beckoning my undivided attention.

Sitting in a sweat lodge in absolute darkness—where the temperature may rise to as much as 105 degrees—listening to the beat of the drum in rhythm with my heartbeat, I found the strength and courage to turn inward. With the help of the elements—air, water, fire and earth—I was taught humility and surrender. Through teachings preserved and passed forward by the Dakota Nation and many other wise and compassionate relatives, and through the practice of meditation and prayer, I was guided toward rediscovering the Oneness of all that is. I had reconnected with all my relations. At last, I found my way home.

I have learned that with patience, practice and time, change will come. Change has come and continues in me with each passing day. I no longer accept the words that echoed so strongly through my very being for so many years of my life and that held me hostage to the belief that I was no good. Today I know better. Today I take full responsibility for my thoughts, words and actions. Today, I can say, "I love myself!"

Mitakuye Oyasin.